PESHARIM

Companion to the Qumran Scrolls, 3

PESHARIM

Timothy H. Lim

SHEFFIELD ACADEMIC PRESS
A Continuum imprint
LONDON • NEW YORK

Published by Sheffield Academic Press Ltd
The Tower Building, 11 York Road, London SE1 7NX
370 Lexington Avenue, New York NY 10017-6550

www.SheffieldAcademicPress.com
www.continuumbooks.com

British Library Cataloguing-in-Publication Data

A catalogue record for this book is available from the British Library

Typeset by Sheffield Academic Press
Printed on acid-free paper in Great Britain by MPG Books, Bodmin, Cornwall

ISBN 1-84127-325-2 (hardback)
       1-84127-273-6 (paperback)

To Laura
'Yet with all this beauty, there is much wisdom in her'
Genesis Apocryphon 20.7

Contents

Preface

While standing together in a queue in Cambridge during the 1995 International Organization for Qumran Studies, I suggested to Philip Davies that it would be useful to have a series of textbooks along the lines of the Old Testament Guides that were intended for senior undergraduates and graduate students. Having benefited from some of the best of the OT guides in teaching Hebrew and Old Testament classes in Edinburgh over the years, I felt that the study of the Qumran scrolls was not well served. I had searched in vain for one or more textbooks that would accompany my honours course on the Dead Sea Scrolls and Christian Origins. Little did I know that this suggestion would lead to an invitation to write one of the volumes.

What I have attempted to do in this book is to write for students with varying backgrounds. Some will have had several years of biblical studies, either of the Hebrew Bible alone or also of the New Testament, alongside intensive language study in biblical Hebrew, Aramaic and/or New Testament Greek, while others would come to it with minimum acquaintance or a survey course. I begin with a general orientation to the scrolls and the pesharim before pursuing important topics in subsequent chapters. I have written the book in a way that provides an introduction for the student and advances the scholarly discussion on the pesharim.

Many thanks to Philip Davies, the general editor of the Companion series, not only for the invitation to contribute, but also for his patience in waiting for the completion of the volume. The delay has meant that I have been able to incorporate several of the texts recently published and edited, and to benefit from important studies by colleagues. The bibliography evidences the centrality of the pesharim in Qumran scholarship. Along the way, I have taken positions on a number of issues, but I have attempted to be fair to my intellectual sparring partners by directing the readers' attention to the relevant publications. It is hoped that by laying out scholarly disagreements students will be led into a deeper engagement with the scrolls and begin to formulate their own views.

I have had the encouragement and support of my immediate and several extended family members. My son and daughter, Jonathan and Alison, are a constant source of joy for their father who marvels at the wonders of their imagination. This book is dedicated to my beloved wife Laura.

Abbreviations

ABD	David Noel Freedman (ed.), *The Anchor Bible Dictionary* (New York: Doubleday, 1992)
BA	*Biblical Archaeologist*
BARev	*Biblical Archaeology Review*
BHS	*Biblia hebraica stuttgartensia*
BO	*Bibliotheca orientalis*
DJD	Discoveries in the Judaean Desert
DSD	*Dead Sea Discoveries*
EDSS	L.H. Schiffmann and J.C. Vanderkam, *Encyclopedia of the Dead Sea Scrolls* (2 vols.; Oxford: Oxford University Press, 2000)
EI	*Eretz Israel*
IDB	George Arthur Buttrick (ed.), *The Interpreter's Dictionary of the Bible* (4 vols.; Nashville: Abingdon Press, 1962)
IDBSup	*IDB*, Supplementary Volume
IEJ	*Israel Exploration Journal*
JBL	*Journal of Biblical Literature*
JJS	*Journal of Jewish Studies*
JNES	*Journal of Near Eastern Studies*
JQR	*Jewish Quarterly Review*
JSJ	*Journal for the Study of Judaism in the Persian, Hellenistic and Roman Period*
JSS	*Journal of Semitic Studies*
MQC	J. Trebolle Barrera and L. Vegas Montaner (eds.), *The Madrid Qumran Congress: Proceedings of the International Congress of the Dead Sea Scrolls, Madrid, 18-21 March 1991* (Leiden: E.J. Brill, 1992)
NTS	*New Testament Studies*
OTS	*Oudtestamentische Studiën*
PAM	Palestine Archaeological Museum (photographic plate number)
RevQ	*Revue de Qumran*
SR	*Studies in Religion/Sciences religieuses*
TZ	*Theologische Zeitschrift*
VT	*Vetus Testamentum*
VTSup	*Vetus Testamentum*, Supplements
WUNT	Wissenschaftliche Untersuchungen zum Neuen Testament
ZNW	*Zeitschrift für die neutestamentliche Wissenschaft*

Editions, Translations and Bibliographies

Editions of the Pesharim and Related Texts

Continuous Pesharim
4QpesherIsaiah^a (4Q161)

Allegro, J.M. and A.A. Anderson
  1968   Qumrân Cave 4. I (4Q158–4Q186) (DJD, 5; Oxford: Clarendon Press): 11-15, pls. IV-V.
  1956   'Further Messianic References in Qumran Literature', *JBL* 75: 177-82, pls. II and III.

Horgan, M.P.
  1979   *Pesharim: Qumran Interpretations of Biblical Books* (Washington: Catholic Biblical Association of America): 70-86; texts: 15-19.

Strugnell, J.
  1969–71   'Notes en marge du volume V des Discoveries in the Judaean Desert of Jordan', *RevQ* 7: 183-86.

4QpesherIsaiah^b (4Q162)
Allegro and Anderson (1968: 15-17, pl. VI).
Horgan (1979: 86-93, texts: 19-20).
Strugnell (1969–71: 186-88).

4QpesherIsaiah^c (4Q163)
Allegro and Anderson (1968: 15-17, pl. VI).
Horgan (1979: 86-93, texts: 19-20).
Strugnell (1969–71: 188-95).

4QpesherIsaiah^d (4Q164)
Allegro and Anderson (1968: 15-17, pl. VI).
Horgan (1979: 86-93, texts: 19-20).
Strugnell (1969–71: 195-96).

4QpesherIsaiah^e (4Q165)
Allegro and Anderson (1968: 15-17, pl. VI).
Horgan (1979: 86-93, texts: 19-20).
Strugnell (1969–71: 197-99).

4QpesherHosea^a (4Q166)
Allegro and Anderson (1968: 15-17, pl. VI).
Horgan (1979: 86-93, texts: 19-20).
Strugnell (1969–71: 199-201).

4QpesherHosea[b] (4Q167)
Allegro and Anderson (1968: 15-17, pl. VI).
Horgan (1979: 86-93, texts: 19-20).
Strugnell (1969–71: 201-203).

1QpesherMicah (1Q14)
Horgan (1979: 55-63, texts: 10-12).
Milik, J.T.
    1955   *Qumran Cave I* (DJD, 1; Oxford: Clarendon Press): 77-80, pl. XV.

4QpesherNahum (4Q169)
Allegro and Anderson (1968: 15-17, pl. VI).
Horgan (1979: 86-93, texts: 19-20).
Strugnell (1969–71: 204-10).

1QpesherHabakkuk
Burrows, M., J.C. Trever and W.H. Brownlee
    1950   *The Dead Sea Scrolls of St Mark's Monastery*. I. *The Isaiah Manuscript and the Habakkuk Pesher* (New Haven: American Schools of Oriental Research).
Horgan (1979: 10-55, texts: 1-9).
Nitzan, B.
    1986   *Pesher Habakkuk: A Scroll from the Wilderness of Judaea (1QpHab)* (Heb.) (Jerusalem: Bialik Institute).

1QpesherZephaniah (1Q15)
Horgan (1979: 63-65, texts: 13-15).
Milik (1955: 80, pl. XV).

1QpesherPsalms (1Q16)
Horgan (1979: 65-70, texts: 13-15).
Milik (1955: 81-82, pl. XV).

4QpesherPsalms[a] (4Q171)
Allegro and Anderson (1968: 15-17, pl. VI).
Horgan (1979: 86-93, texts: 19-20).
Strugnell (1969–71: 211-18).

4QpesherPsalms[b] (4Q173)
Allegro and Anderson (1968: 15-17, pl. VI).
Horgan (1979: 86-93, texts: 19-20).
Strugnell (1969–71: 219-20).

Thematic Pesharim and Texts that Use the Term 'Pesher'

1QWords of Moses (1Q22)
Milik (1955: 91-97, pls. XVIII-XIX).

1QLiturgical Text? (1Q30)
Milik (1955: 132-33, pl. XXX).

4QOrd[a, c] (4Q159 and 4Q153)
Allegro and Anderson (1968: 6-9, pl. II).
Allegro, J.M and A.A. Anderson
    1961   'An Unpublished Fragment of Essene Halakhah (4QOrdinances)', *JSS* 6:
             71-73.
Strugnell (1969–71: 175-79).

4QFlor (4Q174)
Allegro and Anderson (1968: 15-17, pl. VI).
Brooke, G.J.
    1985   *Exegesis at Qumran: 4QFlorilegium in its Jewish Context* (Sheffield: JSOT
             Press).
Steudel, A.
    1994   *Der Midrasch zur Eschatologie aus der Qumrangemeinde (4QMidrEschat[a, b]):*
             Materielle Rekonstruktion, Textebestand, Gattung und traditionsgeschicht-
             liche Einordnung der durk 4Q174 ('Florilegium') und 4Q177 ('Catena A')
             repräsentierten Werkes aus den Qumranfunden (Leiden: E.J. Brill): 5-56.
Strugnell (1969–71: 220-25).

4QCatena[a] (4Q177)
Allegro and Anderson (1968: 67-74, pls. XXIV-XXV).
Steudel (1994: 57-126).
Strugnell (1969–71: 236-48).

4QAges of Creation[a] (4Q180)
Allegro and Anderson (1968: 677-79, pl. XXVII).
Dimant, D.
    1979   'The 'Pesher on the Periods' (4Q180) and 4Q181)', *Israel Oriental*
             Studies 9: 77-102.
Milik, J.T.
    1972   'Milkî-sedeq et Milkî-reša' dans les anciens écrits juifs et chrétiens', *JJS*
             23: 109-26.
Strugnell (1969–71: 252-54).

4QPesher on the Apocalypse of Weeks (4Q247)
Broshi, M. *et al.*
    2000   *Qumran Cave 4.XXVI. Cryptic Texts and Miscellanea, Part 1* (DJD, 36;
             Oxford: Clarendon Press): 187-91.

4QCommentary on Genesis[a] (4Q252)
Brooke, G.J.
    1996   *Qumran Cave 4. XVII: Parabiblical Texts, Part 3* (Oxford: Clarendon
             Press, 1996): 185-207, pls. XII-XIII.

Lim, T.H.
    1992   'The Chronology of the Flood Story in a Qumran Text (4Q252)', *JJS* 43: 288-29.
Stegemann, H.
    1967   'Weitere Stücke von 4QPsalm 37, von 4QPatriarchal Blessings und Hinweis auf eine unedierte Handschrift aus Höhle 4Q mit Exzerpten aus dem Deuteronomium', *RevQ* 6: 211-17.

CD 4.14 (4Q266 frag. 3.1.7)
Baumgarten, J.M.
    1995   'The Damascus Document (CD)', in J.H. Charlesworth (ed.), *The Dead Sea Scrolls: Hebrew, Aramaic, and Greek Texts with English Translations. Damascus Document, War Scroll, and Related Documents* (Tübingen: J.C.B. Mohr [Paul Siebeck]; Louisville, KY: Westminster/John Knox Press): 4-57.
    1996   *Qumran Cave 4. XIII. The Damascus Document (4Q266-273)* (DJD, 18; Oxford: Clarendon Press).
Qimron, E.
    1992   'The Text of CDC', in M. Broshi (ed.), *The Damascus Document Reconsidered* (Jerusalem: Israel Exploration Society/Shrine of the Book): 9-49.
Schechter, S.
    1910   *Documents of Jewish Sectaries.* I. *Fragments of a Zadokite Work* (Cambridge: Cambridge University Press).

4QExposition on the Patriarchs (4Q464)
Eshel, E., and M. Stone
    1993   'The Holy Tongue at the End of Days in Light of a Fragment from Qumran', (Heb.) *Tarbiz* 62: 169-78.
    1995   *Qumran Cave 4. XIV: Parabiblical Texts, Part 2* (DJD, 19; Oxford: Clarendon Press): 215-30, pl. XXIX.

11Melchizedek (11Q13)
García Martínez, F., E.J.C. Tigchelaar and A.S. van der Woude
    1998   *Qumran Cave XI, 11Q2-18, 11Q20-31* (DJD, 23; Oxford: Clarendon Press): 221-41, pl. XXVII.

Other Editions, Tools, Translations and Anthologies
Abegg, M., Jr, P. Flint and E.Ulrich
    1999   *The Dead Sea Scrolls Bible* (New York: HarperSanFrancisco).
Baillet, M.
    1962   *Les 'Petites Grottes' de Qumrân. Exploration de la falise. Les grottes 2Q, 3Q, 5Q, 6Q, 7Q à 10Q. Le rouleau de cuivre* (DJD, 3.1-2; ed. M. Baillet, J.T. Milik and R. de Vaux; Oxford: Clarendon Press). Principal edition of 3Q4.
Baumgarten, J. *et al.*
    1999   *Qumran Cave 4: Halakhic Texts* (DJD, 35; Oxford: Clarendon Press).

Brooke, G.J. with the collaboration of H.K. Bond
  1996   *The Allegro Qumran Collection: Supplement to the Dead Sea Scrolls on Microfiche* (Leiden: E.J. Brill).

Concordance to the Hebrew and Aramaic Fragments from Qumrân Caves II-IX
  1988   Privately published: Göttingen, 1988. Printed from a card index prepared by R.E. Brown, J.A. Fitzmyer, W.G. Oxtoby and J. Teixidor. Prepared and arranged by H.-P. Richter.

Eisenman, R., and J.M. Robinson
  1991   *A Facsimile Edition of the Dead Sea Scrolls* (2 vols.; Washington: Biblical Archaeology Society).

Fitzmyer, J.A.
  1990   *The Dead Sea Scrolls: Major Publication and Tools for Study* (Atlanta: Scholars Press).

García Martínez, F.
  1994–95   *The Dead Sea Scrolls Translated: The Qumran Texts in English* (Leiden: E.J. Brill).

García Martínez, F., and E.J.C. Tigchelaar
  1997–98   *The Dead Sea Scrolls Study Edition. I. (1Q1-4Q273). II. (4Q274-11Q31)* (Leiden: E.J. Brill). Facing Hebrew/Aramaic and English edition.

Gaster, T.H.
  1976   *The Dead Sea Scriptures in English Translation* (Garden City, NY: Doubleday, 3rd edn).

Habermann, A.M.
  1952   *'edah we-'eduth. Three Scrolls from the Judaean Desert: The Legacy of a Community* (Heb.) (Jerusalem: Mahbaroth le-Sifruth).

Knibb, M.
  1987   *The Qumran Community* (Cambridge: Cambridge University Press). Contains translated extracts with commentary on some of the most important scrolls.

Kuhn, K.G. *et al.*
  1958   *Rückläufiges Hebräisches Wörterbuch* (Göttingen: Vandenhoeck & Ruprecht).
  1960   *Konkordanz zu den Qumrantexten.* (Göttingen: Vandenhoeck & Ruprecht). Plus supplements in *RevQ* 4 (1963–64): 163-234.

Lim, T.H. in consultation with P.S. Alexander
  1997   *The Dead Sea Scrolls Electronic Reference Library Volume 1* (Oxford: Oxford University Press; Leiden: E.J. Brill). Digitized images of all the Dead Sea Scrolls with bibliographical annotations.

Lohse, E.
  1964   *Die Texte aus Qumran: Hebräisch und deutsch* (Munich: Kösel-Verlag). Facing Hebrew (with masoretic pointing) and German texts.

Maier, J.
  1960   *Die Texte vom Toten Meer* (2 vols.; Basel/Munich: Ernst Reinhardt Verlag).

Puèch, E.
  1987   'Konkordanz zu XIQMelkîsédeq', *RevQ* 12: 515-18.

Reed, S.A.
  1994   *The Dead Sea Scrolls Catalogue: Documents, Photographs and Museum*

Inventory Numbers (Rev. M.J. Lundberg and M.B. Phelps; Atlanta: Scholars Press).

Sukenik, E.L.
1955   *The Dead Sea Scrolls of the Hebrew University* (prepared by N. Avigad and Y. Yadin; Jerusalem: Magnes Press).

Tov, E. (ed.)
1999   *The Dead Sea Scrolls Electronic Reference Library*. Volume 2. Prepared by the Foundation for Ancient Research and Mormon Studies. Including 'The Dead Sea Scrolls Database (Non-Biblical Texts) (Leiden: E.J. Brill Academic Publishers).

Tov, E. with the collaboration of S.J. Pfann
1993   *The Dead Sea Scrolls on Microfiche* (Leiden: E.J. Brill).

Vermes, G.
1987   *The Dead Sea Scrolls in English* (London: Penguin Books, 3rd edn).
1997   *The Complete Dead Sea Scrolls in English* (London: Penguin Books, 5th edn).

Wacholder, B.Z. and M.G. Abegg
1991–95   *A Preliminary Edition of the Unpublished Dead Sea Scrolls* (3 vols.; Washington: Biblical Archaeology Society).

Wise, M., M. Abegg and E. Cook
1996   *The Dead Sea Scrolls: A New Translation* (San Francisco: HarperSanFrancisco). Recent English translation on the scrolls.

Yadin, Y.
1983   *The Temple Scroll* (2 vols.; Jerusalem: Israel Exploration Society).

1

INTRODUCTION

1. The Dead Sea Scrolls and the Qumran Scrolls

The Dead Sea Scrolls can refer broadly to all the ancient manuscripts discovered in the modern age in the Judaean Wilderness up and down the western side of the Dead Sea, or they can designate specifically those scrolls and fragments first unearthed in 1947 in the eleven caves situated on the hillside surrounding the north-western corner of 'the Sea of Salt' (*yam ha-melaḥ*). The latter, narrower definition, which will be used here, most commonly assumes that these 800 plus ancient texts are related to the archaeological site of Khirbet ('ruin of') Qumran and to the monastic-like Jewish sect of the Essenes.

Both these assumptions, however, have been challenged. Two scholars argue that these scrolls have neither a direct relationship to the archaeological site, which they argue was a military fortress, nor to the Jewish sect of the Essenes known primarily through descriptions in the classical writings of Philo, Josephus and Pliny. According to this 'Jerusalem hypothesis' these scrolls were sequestered to the Judaean Wilderness from Jerusalem and its libraries when the inhabitants of the Holy City heard of the fall of Galilee and of the approaching Roman army. Fearful that these treasures and writings would be taken as booty of war or destroyed, the Jerusalemites hid these precious possessions in the Judaean Wilderness some 25–30 miles eastwards. These scrolls, therefore, represent the range of beliefs of ancient Palestinian Judaism, and not simply the narrow theological and legal concerns of one marginal sect.

This 'Jerusalem hypothesis', first proposed in the early 1960s by Karl Rengstorff (1960), and more recently advanced independently by Norman Golb (1995) has not had many supporters. It is fair to say that most scholars are persuaded by the connection of the scrolls to the Qumran archaeological site, because the majority of the caves (4–10) are situated near the ruins. The proximity of the site and caves is not accidental. Moreover, these caves are related to ones further north (Caves 1–3 and 11) by the copies of the same scrolls that were found in them. For instance, copies of the *Community Rule*, once known as the *Manual of Discipline*, have been found in 'the backyard' of the archaeological ruin, in Caves 4 and 5, as well as in Cave 1, approximately two-thirds of a mile north of Qumran (cf. Lim, 1992a: pp. 456-61).

Another way by which some of the scrolls have been dissociated from the Qumran site is by the postulate of a tradition of forming letters and spelling peculiar to the Qumran community and by noting the languages in which these scrolls were written. According to Emanuel Tov (1986) there exists a system of Qumran orthography, or more accurately morphology, that is characterized by full spelling. Using consonants such as 'mothers of reading' (*matres lectionis*), many of the scrolls, written in unpointed Hebrew, adopted 'helps' by marking implicit vowels with consonants. For example, a final syllable that is to be pronounced with *a* can be represented by attaching *h* to the end of a word, thus pronounced as *hu'ah* ('he, it').

Those scrolls that were written in this system of writing, Tov argued, were copied at Qumran by the community that lived there, whereas other scrolls that reflect a different morphology were thought to have been transcribed elsewhere and subsequently brought to the sectarian desert centre. Tov also held that the scrolls found in Cave 7 must have been imported into the community, since all of them were written in Greek, rather than in Hebrew or Aramaic, and they do not reflect sectarian ideology.

The plausibility of Tov's views is dependent upon the persuasiveness of his identification of the so-called Qumran orthography. Some would question the distinctiveness of this system of writing and Frank Cross would prefer to describe it more generally as the phenomenon of baroque spelling (1992: 7). On the distinctive features of the scrolls from Cave 7, it has to be admitted that an explanation is needed for the presence of only Greeks texts, but the theory that these were imported into the community remains no more than a possibility. Perhaps volunteers who joined the community brought with them scrolls that were written in Greek.

Was the decision to deposit them in Cave 7 rather than in another one really dependent upon the language, provenance and sectarian concerns of the scrolls? If so, why is this not borne out in, say, Cave 4, where Greek, Hebrew and Aramaic texts of the Bible, Apocrypha, Pseudepigrapha and sectarian writings lay side by side? Alternatively, it may be an accident of history that Greek texts survived the ravages of time. After all, there are too few badly mutilated texts found in this 'little cave' to draw any far-reaching conclusion about the original linguistic composition of the corpus, its place of origin or what the Qumran community thought of it.

Attempts, then, to dissociate the scrolls from the archaeological site of Qumran have met with mixed success. On the other hand the recent discovery of an ostracon containing 'a deed of gift' on the plateau of the site has not provided the decisive evidence either for connecting the scrolls to Qumran. In the vital line 8 of that document, Frank Moore Cross and Esther Eshel (1997: 18) read the broken and faded words as a reference to the completion of a certain Honi's initiation procedure: 'when he fulfils (his oath) to the *yaḥad*'. The term *yaḥad*, in biblical Hebrew meaning 'union' or 'association', has become one of the favoured self-designations by the sectarians and is now considered a technical term in Qumran scholarship.

The transcription of this term, however, has been challenged by Ada Yardeni (1998) who read and divided the contentious letters differently: instead of a *yod* she read a *nun* and interpreted it as the final letter of the Hebrew word for 'tree' (*'yln*); the second letter she transcribed as *aleph* rather than *het* and the third a *het* rather than a *dalet*. In Yardeni's view, line 8 would read 'and every oth[er] tree' and this would be seen as following on the description of the estate and all its trees that Honi bequeathed to someone named El'azar. Cross and Eshel have now replied (DJD, 36).

The controversial reading of the 'gift of deed' notwithstanding, it has to be said that most scholars are still convinced by the relationship of the scrolls to the adjoining ruins. The sheer proximity of the caves to the archaeological site and the undeniable association of copies of the same texts from different caves remain powerful arguments for seeing the scrolls as most probably related to Qumran.

But in what ways are the scrolls, caves and archaeological site related? It is helpful to think of the scrolls as belonging to the 'library' of the community that once lived on the Qumran site. The comparison with the 'library', like most analogies, is only partial and imperfect. There is no evidence of a reference system or loan-periods such as found in modern institutions. It is a 'library' in the sense that the collection was gathered from various sources, some works of which were composed by members of the community while others, like copies of the biblical texts, belong generally to Judaism of the late Second Temple period.

The Dead Sea Scrolls, in this narrow sense of the phrase, refer to the heterogeneous collection of scrolls found in the eleven caves that served as depositories for the Qumran community. Given the above considerations, they will continue to be used here to designate 'the Qumran scrolls'.

2. The Essenes and the Qumran Community

What of the Essenes? Are they to be identified with the Qumran community described in the scrolls? For a time in the history of scholarship, it was axiomatic that the Essenes were none other than members of the Qumran community. The reigning hypothesis was the 'Maccabean theory' that not only identified the Qumran community with the Essenes, but also purported to see in the insult of 'the Wicked Priest' and 'the Liar' a coded reference to Jonathan or Simon Maccabee. According to this theory, the Qumran Essenes separated themselves from the Jerusalem centre of worship because of the illegitimate accession to the high priesthood of Jonathan or Simon Maccabee, neither of whom was a Zadokite.

While much more will be said below about these historical identifications, it should be noted from the outset that recent scholarship has queried many of these cherished beliefs and has formulated rather differently the question of the origin and history of the Qumran community. According to the Dutch view of Florentino García Martínez (a Spanish scholar working in the Netherlands) and the late Adam van der Woude, the Essene movement had two daughter sects, one the Qumran community and the other the Therapeutae in Egypt (García Martínez and van der Woude 1990). This Groningen hypothesis has the advantage of explaining the affinities between the Qumran community and another Egyptian Jewish sect, the Therapeutae, as well as their differences. The weaknesses of this theory will be discussed below, particularly in relation to the historical identifications of six wicked priests.

Lawrence H. Schiffman (1994), following on the ground breaking studies of Solomon Schechter and Louis Ginzberg on the 'Zadokite Fragments' from the Cairo Genizah and Joseph Baumgarten's study of ritual purity in the Qumran scrolls, has advanced a theory of the Sadducean origins of the Qumran community well beyond the views of his predecessors. Based on the recently published text called 'Some Precepts of the Torah' (the title is taken from the first significant line of the document and has the sigla 4QMMT) from Cave 4, Schiffman argues that certain legal positions concerning impurities and ritual washings agree with views attributed to the Sadducees in Rabbinic literature, and that this 'we-party' is none other than the nascent Qumran community. Joseph Baumgarten, however, has countered with the observation that the halakhic parallels between the scrolls and Essenes are more impressive than those found between the scrolls and those attributed to the Sadducees in the Mishnah (1992: 503-504). Schiffman has yet to reply fully, but he has indicated that Baumgarten has not given sufficient weight to the Sadducean parallels (2000: 140 n. 86).

The subject of the origin and history of the Qumran community is broader than the present discussion of the sectarian biblical commentaries. Nevertheless, it is worth noting that recent scholarship has tended to be more careful in describing the Qumran community as a monolithic entity.

Already in antiquity, Josephus distinguished two orders of the Essenes, the celibate and the married (*War* 2.120, 160). Philip Davies (1996: 139-50) has stressed the distinction between the *yaḥad* and other groups described in the scrolls. Whether these are different groups or one group that evolved over time remains an unresolved question. In any case, it is surely to be expected that any community, like the Qumran one, that lasted for some 220 years (between c. 150 BCE and 70 CE) should experience development and change. Tracing this process is the subject of another book.

3. The Study of the Scrolls and Confessionalism

Has Qumran scholarship been guilty of christianizing the scrolls? Lawrence Schiffman has argued that the Dead Sea Scrolls need to be reclaimed for Judaism, since the past 50 years have seen an almost exclusive focus on the significance of the scrolls for a better understanding of the early Church. His work, first published in 1994 with the provocative title *Reclaiming the Dead Sea Scrolls*, purports to be 'the first work ever written to explain their [i.e. the scrolls'] significance in understanding the history of Judaism' (p. xiii). This is a bold claim.

Schiffman's objections against the use of Christian terminology do, however, raise important issues about how one might describe the Qumran community. He pointed out that the members of the community were not monks, led by a Teacher of Righteousness and bishop, who performed baptisms, ate in a refectory, and copied manuscripts in their scriptorium, but were observant Jews, guided by a Rabbi and a Teacher of Righteousness, who performed ritual purifications in the *mikveh* or ritual bath, ate communal meals and copied texts in their library (1994: 18). It has to be admitted that by describing the Qumran community in this way, Schiffman has dramatically altered the perception of the desert sectarians. But has he really succeeded in reclaiming the scrolls for Judaism?

Is it not also anachronistic and inappropriate to depict the Qumran community in terms of Rabbinic Judaism? For example, should the laws be described as halakhah, a technical term used variously in Rabbinic literature for legal debates and judgments? Some would prefer using the more neutral *mishpatim* or laws. Of course the term 'halakhah' can be used for heuristic purposes if one defines it. It could be argued that while one is aware that the term postdates this historical period, it usefully serves to identify certain features of Qumran teaching and to underscore the continuity of Jewish legal discourse.

But if this is so, then why cannot terminology derived from Christian tradition, likewise qualified, be used to describe features found in later monastic tradition? Terminology applied in this way is equally apt and inappropriate. The Greek term *monasterion*, which is the etymological root of the English word 'monastery', is even used by Philo to describe the room into which the Therapeutae would retreat for reflection and private study (*Vit. Cont.* 25). This is not to say that Philo meant 'monastery' by *monasterion*, but that the term adopted by Christian ascetic tradition was the same word earlier used to describe the Therapeutae's 'small room'.

Whether it is in the biological classification of new species, the textual description of biblical scrolls, or the historical description of a sect, the descriptive process moves from the known to the unknown. The real issue, it seems, is not about the use of this or that term, unless one is unaware of its limitations, but the claim of the Qumran community for confessional and ideological biases, whether intentionally or unconsciously: to do so intentionally is self-serving and produces bad history. No one approaches historical writing in an entirely neutral and objective fashion, as postmodernists are wont to remind us, yet subjectivity can be kept in check by reflection and the distancing of the historian from the subject. Schiffman has raised our awareness of how we study the Dead Sea Scrolls and it is this important point that one must take on board more than the alternative of seeing the Qumran community through the lens of Rabbinic Judaism.

4. A Community of Study

Seeing the Qumran Community for itself is not only historically more defensible, but it also has several advantages. The Qumran community was a bookish association that sought inspiration from certain authoritative writings. It was 'bookish' in the sense that it believed that divine will can be found in an inspired reading of texts. But it was not 'bookish' in the literal sense that it read from *books* (i.e. codices) or that it had a well-defined canon of Holy Scriptures on which to comment as in later Rabbinic Judaism. They studied individual scrolls for the most part and while there was clearly a core group of authoritative texts, comprising the Torah, most of the prophets and some of the writings, there was no 'Qumran Bible' in the canonical sense of the term as expressed in the flawed title of *The Dead Sea Scrolls Bible* (cf. 2001a: Lim).

If the act of citing or alluding to a text is any indication of authoritative status, then it can be argued that the Qumran community also revered Jubilees, Enoch and the Temple Scroll in the same way that they considered authoritative other works that eventually found their way into the canon of the Bible. For in the sectarian writings quotations were drawn not only from 'biblical books', but also from extra-canonical works.

5. The Pesharim

The *pesharim* are some of the best-known biblical exegeses to be found among the Dead Sea Scrolls. They are scriptural commentaries named after the technical Hebrew term *pesher* (pl. *pesharim*) which characteristically appears in formulae that introduce an exposition of a biblical verse (e.g., 'the intepretation [Hebrew: *pesher*] of the matter is...'). This particular genre of exegesis figures prominently in almost all textbooks on the Qumran scrolls and has been sensationalized by Barbara Thiering as the interpretative 'key' to unlocking the putative mystery behind such ancient texts as the New Testament Gospels (Thiering 1992) and the book of Revelation (Thiering 1996). Despite popularity among lay readers, Thiering has found little support among the scholarly guild.

'Too much familiarity breeds contempt' admonishes the common proverb and for some the popularity of the *pesharim* does breed a false sense of contempt over material that seems just too familiar. It is false because it is a mistake to suppose that the prominence of a subject means that it is well understood or that a passing acquaintance (as is often the case) with one or two *pesharim* constitutes familiarity with the genre.

Moreover, recently published texts (e.g. 4Q252) raise fundamental questions as to the character of the *pesher* and its relationship to other forms of biblical interpretation. What is a *pesher*? For many, it is that form of exegesis, practised by the Qumran community that identifies events and people in the biblical texts with contemporary historical figures. What most readily come to mind are the *Habakkuk Pesher*, the *Nahum Pesher* and notable passages from the *Psalms Pesher* (e.g. on Ps. 37). But acquaintance with only these, or purple passages found within them, is insufficient for a thorough understanding of the exegetical methods and hermeneutical principles.

The centrality of the *pesharim* in Qumran study poses another problem and this is the sheer volume of scholarly output. Debates about the identity of the Teacher of Righteousness, the Wicked Priest (or priests), the Liar and the use of a different calendar often turn on a particular reading of passages from the *pesharim*. Was Jonathan or Simon Maccabee the historical figure known in the scrolls by his negative sobriquet 'the Wicked Priest'? Or should 'the wicked priest' be understood as the title of a succession of high priests whom the Qumran community regarded as morally depraved? Is 'the liar' another name for 'the Wicked Priest' or is it an epithet that the Qumran community coined to disparage a competing teacher of the law? Did the Teacher of Righteousness send a legal document to the Wicked Priest and is that work the Temple Scroll or the treatise known as 4QMMT (4 = Cave 4;

Q = Qumran; MMT = 'miqsat ma'se hatorah' or 'some precepts of the torah')? Is the explanation of the Wicked Priest's ability to travel on Yom Kippur to be found in the use of divergent calendars in the Qumran community and at the official Jerusalem cultus?

It is perhaps an exaggeration, but maybe only slightly so, to say that the scholarly publications on the pesharim alone can fill a small library. For the uninitiated student and reader, becoming familiar with this substantial body of scholarly publications is a daunting task. Some students experience a kind of intellectual paralysis, brought on by the anxiety of saying anything at all in the presence of so much previously published material.

6. Types of Pesharim

One way of beginning study of these Qumran compositions is to distinguish between those pesherite texts that comment sequentially on larger and smaller sections of a biblical book from other interpretations that are arranged around a theme. Even though pesherite exegesis is more complex than this dual classification, as will be seen, Jean Carmignac's categorization of the continuous pesher (*pesher continu*) and thematic pesher (*pesher thématique*) does draw a useful line between those texts that provide a running commentary on the biblical texts and those that group scriptural proof-texts according to a central idea (1969–71: 342-78).

Examples of the latter include 11QMelchizedek (11Q13), a text that describes the redemptive work of the mysterious figure of the heavenly Melchizedek by the exegesis of a clutch of biblical texts, namely Lev. 25.9, 13; Deut. 15.2; Isa. 52.7, 61.1-3; Ps. 7.7-9, 82.1-2; and Dan. 9.25. Here, the technical term '*pesher*' appears in some of the introductory formulae.

Similarly, 4QFlorilegium (4Q174) introduces (with the requisite technical term) and interprets its collection of biblical proof-texts that consists of 2 Sam. 7.10-14; Isa. 8.11; Ezek. 44.10; Dan. 12.10; and Ps. 1.1, 2.1. Together these biblical texts are understood to point to the sectarian ideology of an eschatological Temple and the messianic figures of the branch of David and the interpreter of the law.

John Allegro published 30 fragments of a text under the title of 4QCatena[a] (Allegro and Anderson 1968: 67-74). 'Catena' is a term used to describe a series of connected comments on Scripture in patristic literature. John Strugnell expressed reservations about using the title 'catena' or even 'florilegium' and observed that the text is characterized by the phrase *be'aḥarit ha-yamim* or 'at the end of days' and its historical realization of certain biblical passages (1969–71: 236). He noted a pattern of using the first or subsequent verses of a number of Psalms (6.2-3, 6; 11.1; 12.1, 7; 13.2-3, 5; 16.3; 17.1) and intermingled with other allusions and citations to other biblical texts and ancient historical events (e.g. Abraham, Joshua and Jacob). He also reported that P.W. Skehan had drawn his attention to the parallel structure of the *midrash* on Psalm 1 and 2 in 4Q174.

Following Strugnell's comments, it has recently been argued by Annette Steudel that 4Q174 belongs together with 4Q177 to a composition that interprets the fate of the righteous and wicked at the end of days, a kind of eschatological midrash (1994: 57-160). While such a reconstruction is possible, the lack of textual overlap between the two documents means that this suggestion remains no more than a possibility. The obvious alternative is to consider 4Q174 and 4Q177 as copies of two distinct, albeit similar types of, exegeses.

The arrangement of the continuous *pesher* by contrast is much more straightforward. The consecutive comments of the exegesis follow the perceived sense units of the biblical texts. Some of these divisions do correspond to the later versification of the masoretes as found in the traditional Hebrew Bible, but others do not do so. At its most basic, the form of the exegesis is: biblical citation (or lemma), introductory formula (frequently including, though not invariably, the term *pesher*), and its comment on the verse. This is followed by the quotation and interpretation of the next sense unit and so on until the end of the passage.

7. Pesherite Biblical Quotations

There are fifteen texts that belong to the *pesher* of the continuous kind: five commentaries on Isaiah, seven on minor prophet books (Habakkuk, Nahum, Micah, Zephaniah and Hosea), and three on the Psalms. Three other texts have sometimes been counted among them, given that the one probably mentions 'the [d]ay of judgme[nt]' (3QpIsa [3Q4]), another attests to the interpretative formula 'and concerning' (4QCommentary on Malachi [4Q253a]), and the third to an 'Apocalypse of Weeks' (4Q247), but none of the fragments contain the technical term, and eschatological orientation alone does not define a text in the strict sense as a *pesher*. Curiously, Berrin claims that the text called 'pesher on the true Israel' (4Q239), along with 1Q30, contain the 'the word pesher but are too fragmentary to characterize' (2000: 646). Although 4Q239 is indeed listed in the official catalogue by Tov (1993: 37), there is no PAM number or any information of its whereabouts. There is no entry for it either in the latest database edited by Tov in *The Dead Sea Scrolls Electronic Reference Library* (1999).

Under the sigla 4Q172 (4QpUnidentified), John Allegro had assembled 14 fragments that may have originally belonged to one or more pesharim (1968: 50-51) . Of these, John Strugnell (1969–71: 218) has reassigned fragment 10 and Maurya Horgan (1979: 263-65) fragment 1 to 4QpPs³ (4Q171). On palaeographical grounds, fragment 5 of 4QpPsᵇ (4Q173) does not belong together with the other four fragments (Strugnell 1969–71: 219). It belongs to a different text and it may be a pesher, but the technical term is not preserved. 4Q182 (4QCatenaᵇ) may also be a pesher on Jeremiah, based upon its eschatological perspective, but the term is not preserved.

The biblical verses quoted by these fifteen pesharim are listed below (not including allusions):

4QpIsaᵃ (4Q161): Isa. 10.22, 24-34, 11.1-5
4QpIsaᵇ (4Q162): Isa. 5.5-6, 11-14, 24-25, 29-30
4QpIsaᶜ (4Q163): Isa. 8.7-8; 9.11, 13-20; 10.12, 19-24; 14.8, 26-30; 19.9-12; 29.10-11, 15-16, 18-23; 30.1-5, 15-21, 23; 31.1. Also Zech. 11.11, Hos. 6.9a and possibly a reference to Jeremiah.
4QpIsaᵈ (4Q164): Isa. 54.11-12
4QpIsaᵉ (4Q165): Isa. 11.11-12; 14.19; 15.4-5; 21.10-11, 13, 15; 32.5-7; 40.12
4QpHosᵃ (4Q166): Hos. 2.8-14
4QpHosᵇ (4Q167): Hos. 5.13-15; 6.4, 7, 9-11; 8.6-7, 13-14
1QpMic (1Q14): Mic. 1.2-6, 9; 6.15-16
4QpNah (4Q169): Nah. 1.3-6, 2.12-14; 3.1-12, 14
1QpHab: Hab. 1.2-2.20
1QpZeph (1Q15): Zeph. 1.18-2.2
4QpZeph (4Q170): Zeph. 1.12-13
1QpPs (1Q16): Ps. 68.13, 26-27, 30-31
4QpPsᵃ (4Q171): Ps. 37.2, 5-26, 28-30, 32-40; 45.1-2; 60.8-9
4QpPsᵇ (4Q173): Ps. 129.7-8

The thematic pesharim and other related texts interpret the following biblical verses by using the technical term.

1. *1QWords of Moses* (1Q22): the partially preserved root *pšr* is read by J. T. Milik (DJD, I, pp. 91-97) in col. 1, line 3 as an imperative: 'interpret!' According to him God commanded Moses to interpret the words of the law to the heads of the families, levites and priests, but merely notify the commandments to the people.
2. *1QLiturgical Text?* (1Q30): preserves the term 'pesher' and it is possible that it is interpreting a verse from the Pentateuch or the Psalter (cf. 'five-part books', so Milik, DJD, I, pp. 132-33), but it is too badly mutilated to identify what this verse may be.
3. *4QOrdᵃ, ᵇ, ᶜ* (4Q159 and 4Q153; it is uncertain whether 4Q154 is related since there is no overlap with the former two): the term *pesher* apparently follows two quotations (frag 5), but the biblical sources have not been identified (possibly from Lev. 16.1, so Allegro and Anderson 1968: 9). The commentaries re-interpret

various biblical laws derived from Deut. 23.25-26; Exod. 30.11-16; Lev. 25.39-46; and Lev. 23. Recently, Baumgarten has suggested that 4Q159 is a medley of biblical laws akin to 4Q265 and its interpretation alludes to sins resulting from the golden calf episode in Exodus 32 (1999: 58-59).

4. *4QFlor* (4Q174): Ps. 1.1 (introduced by the term 'midrash' and followed by 'pesher') and Ps. 2.1. Other biblical quotations cited, but without the accompanying technical term included: Ps. 89.2, 2 Sam. 7.10, Exod. 15.17-18, 2 Sam. 7.11, 12-14, Amos 9.11, Isa. 8.11, Ezek. 44.10, Dan. 12.10/11.32.

5. *4QCatena* (4Q177 following Steudel 1994: 71-124): Ps. 13.2-3 and 17.1. Other biblical texts cited are Isa. 37.30, 32.7 Ps. 11.1-2, Mic. 2.10-11, Ps. 12.1, Isa. 22.13, 27.11, Ps. 12.7, Zech. 3.9, Isa. 6.10, Ezek. 25.8, Deut. 7.15, Ps. 16.3, Nah. 2.11, Hos. 5.8, Jer. 18.18, and Ps. 6.2-3, 4-5.

6. *4QAgesCreat* (4Q180), also known as 'Pesher on the Periods' (after Dimant 1979): the technical term 'pesher' is used twice to introduce the concept of ages which God had made and Azazel and the angels who consorted with the daughters of man (cf. Gen. 6.4). The term is plausibly reconstructed in the formula '[the interpretation] of the word' as a comment on Gen. 18.20-21.

7. *4QCommentary on Genesis* (4Q252): the technical term occurs only once in an interpretative formula for Gen. 49.3-4. The six columns of this text are replete with verbatim quotations or close paraphrases from Gen. 7.10–8.13, 9.24-27, 22.10-12, and Deut. 25.19. Interestingly, Gen. 49.10 is cited in the manner of the pesher without using the technical term (Lim 2000b: 64). 4Q254 and 4Q254a are related to this text.

8. *CD 4.14* (cf. 4Q266): an interpretative formula using the word 'pesher' introduces a commentary on Isa. 24.17 that forms a central passage in the Damascus Document. The Admonitions is, of course, replete with biblical passages, both quoted in verbatim and by allusion. The most important ones that support the exposition on 'the three nets of Belial' are Mic. 2.16, Gen. 1.27, 7.9, Deut. 17.17 and Lev. 18.13.

9. *4QExposition on the Patriarchs* (4Q464): the term 'pesher' is used to interpret a quotation of Gen. 15.13 (Eshel and Stone 1995: 215-30).

10. *11QMelch* (11Q13): the pesher-formula introduces the comment on Ps. 82.2 and Isa. 52.7. This eschatological interpretation, centering on the supernatural figure of Melchizedek and his redemptive act in the end-time, quotes a number of other biblical

texts, including Lev. 25.13, Deut. 15.21, Ps. 82.1, Ps. 7.8-9 and Lev. 25.9 (García Martínez, Tigchelaar and van der Woude 1998: 221-41).

In the past, scholars have tended to assume that the biblical text as reconstituted from the quotations can be textually characterized as an early example of the Masoretic Text (MT), the so-called proto-Masoretic Text, despite having numerous readings that differ from the standard Hebrew Bible. A reading that varies from the MT is understood as an exegetical variant rather than a textual variant. The pesherist apparently created this variant by modifying the words of Scripture to suit his interpretation.

Recently, there has been an attempt to reconsider the textual nature of the pesherite biblical quotations. In a study published in 1997 (*Holy Scripture in the Qumran Commentaries and Pauline Letters*), I raised the issue of the textual classification of the pesherite biblical texts in relation to exegesis. Two main considerations led me to reconsider the common assumption that the proto-Masoretic Text lay before the pesherist as he copied and then interpreted the biblical oracles.

First, studies on the Qumran biblical texts show that in this period (c. 300 BCE to 100 CE) Jewish authoritative writings remained canonically open and more importantly textually fluid. There was recognition that certain books had a special status, but this list of authoritative writings was not closed. Moreover, this canonical openness was accompanied by a lack of textual fixity. Although the degree of textual fluidity differed from book to book of the Hebrew Bible, the variation was more significant than spelling differences.

The pre-Qumran view of textual criticism was of two or three text-types of the Hebrew Bible. The MT, Samaritan Pentateuch (SP) and the Septuagint (LXX) represented the three text-types of the first five books, and either two (MT and LXX) or three (including the SP by analogy) text-types are represented in the remaining books. In the past 50 years, there has been a growing recognition that the tri-or bi-partite classification of the biblical texts is inadequate in accounting for the evidence of the scrolls. Emanuel Tov, for instance, saw a multiplicity of textual traditions extant in Second Temple Judaism, even though he considered the base-text of the pesharim to be proto-MT.

Secondly, given this growing recognition of textual diversity, it is much more difficult to know whether the pesherist altered his biblical text by adapting original readings identical with the MT or by simply using a version of the biblical book that already contained these variants. Did the interpretation generate the variant or the variant the interpretation?

8. Editing Scrolls

The thematic and continuous *pesharim* are found in three caves both near the Khirbet Qumran site (Cave 4) and further north (Caves 1 and 11). The editing of these scrolls is notoriously complex. To begin with, not all the pesharim are well preserved like the Habakkuk Pesher that contains most of the original thirteen columns. Most of them are fragmentary remains of texts rather than whole scrolls or a few columns from them.

Using a method of studying ancient handwriting known as palaeography, the original international team and subsequent editors collected all the fragments of the same script on one or more plates and joined pieces that had matching edges. Where two or more fragments are correctly joined, it can safely be assumed that these originally belonged to the same text. Added to these are other fragments that have no matching edges while exhibiting the same handwriting and content.

Errors can creep into this procedure of reconstructing mutilated texts in several ways. An editor may be mistaken in his identification of two similar, but distinct, handwritings, since scribes learned how to form their letters according to schools and convention. For example, John Allegro collected five unconnected fragments under the title 4QpPs[b] (4Q173) (Allegro and Anderson 1968: 51-53). In a review of the volume, John Strugnell (1969–71: p. 219) agreed that the first four fragments belong to a second pesher on the Psalms from Cave 4, but questioned the inclusion of fragment five on palaeographical grounds—namely, that it was written by another scribe. He dated the script of the latter to a half century later in the Herodian period and argued that fragment five may not be a pesher at all, but a unique text that happens to quote Ps. 118.20. In her study of all the pesharim, Horgan (1979: 226) followed Strugnell.

It would seem that this is a straightforward case of an editor making a palaeographical error. But it is not quite so simple. More than one scribe could be responsible for the transcription of a scroll. For example, the virtually intact *Habakkuk Pesher* was copied by two scribes of the Herodian period. As Karl Elliger (1953: 72-74) noted long ago, the first scribe copied col. 1.1–12.13 and the second scribe columns 12.13-13.4. Had the *Habakkuk Pesher* not been preserved so extensively, but was found in tatters, then a suggestion that these pieces originally belonged to two texts because they were copied by different scribes would clearly be wrong.

Palaeography alone is not decisive in this case and the extant content of fragment five is too paltry to be conclusive. However, it does cite Psalm 118. Was the original, intact scroll copied by two different scribes, one stopped at the end of the interpretation of Psalm 118 and the other beginning with

Psalm 129? The textual distance between these two psalms in the traditional enumeration can be explained either by the skipping of intervening psalms as in 4QpPs[a] or by a different order (cf. Ps. 118 is found between Pss. 116 and 104 [in that order] in 11QPs[a]).

This is not to say that Allegro was correct in including fragment five in 4Q173, but to illustrate the difficulties faced by the editor in the absence of an extant exemplar. Concerning another *pesher*, both Allegro (1968: 17-27) and Strugnell (1969–71: 188–95) regarded the 57 (the latter added four other) fragments of 4QpIsa[c] (4Q163) as having been copied by two different scribes.

An associated problem is that a scribe did copy more than one text in his lifetime. For example, Strugnell noted that the same scribe or school was responsible for 4QpIsa[a] (4Q161), 4QpHos[a] (4Q166) and 4QpPs[a] (4Q171) (Strugnell 1969–71: 183 n. 17). Now the quotation of different biblical books of Isaiah, Hosea and Psalms would give the editor strong grounds for separating the non-contiguous fragments into three groups, but it would be less easy if the source is the same biblical text (see now George Brooke's separation of fragments of Genesis into two distinct commentaries, 4Q254 and 4Q254a, in DJD, 22, p. 233).

9. Dating the Pesharim

Some of the scrolls have been dated by palaeographical and radiocarbon methods. As was mentioned above, the study of ancient handwriting or palaeography aids the editor in his or her task of grouping non-contiguous fragments together. But it also serves to date a scroll by fixing its point along a typological sequence of script development. Frank Cross (1961) has developed a palaeographical dating sequence that divides the Qumran scripts into three distinct periods: archaic (250–150 BCE), Hasmonaean (150–30 BCE), and Herodian (30 BCE–70 CE). An approximate date within an accuracy of 25 years can be suggested by aligning the scribal hand of an individual scroll along this continuum. Nahman Avigad (1958: 72) has cautioned against the assignment of absolute dates for the Herodian group of scrolls, since it is unknown how quickly the forms of individual letters developed.

Recently this method of dating the scrolls has been complemented by two radiocarbon tests conducted in 1990 and 1994 respectively at the Zurich Institut für Mittelenergiephysik (Bonani *et al.* 1991) and the Arizona Accelerator Mass Spectromerty Facility (Jull *et al.* 1996) that broadly confirmed the palaeographical dates. As was recognized, there was a need to fix the entire typology with external criteria, since the Qumran scrolls do not contain internal dates and the palaeographical estimates depended upon the relative sequence of script development.

Thirty-two texts were sampled in these tests and two *pesharim*, namely the Habakkuk Pesher (1QpHab) and 4QpPs^a (4Q171), were subjected to the Accelerator Mass Spectrometry (AMS) procedure in Arizona. The results showed that 1QpHab has a calibrated age of 104–43 BCE in the one standard deviation range of confidence and of 120–125 BCE (97%) in the two sigma range. These radiocarbon dates match the palaeographical date of 30–31 BCE of the early Herodian hand.

The results for 4QpPs^a showed dates of 22–78 CE and 5–111 CE in the one and two standard deviation ranges of confidence respectively. Jull *et al.* have not noted the palaeographical date (1996: 88, Table 2), but it can be deduced from Strugnell's notes. Strugnell described 4Q171 as having been written either by the same scribe or another scribe of the same school who produced 4Q161 and 4Q166 (1969–71: 183 and n. 17). He further characterized the latter's scribal hand as a developed Herodian script (p. 199), presumably dating it to the latter part of the 30 BCE to 70 CE range, say from 20–70 CE. This matches well the radiocarbon estimates.

Information on the dates of the pesharim is incomplete. The following is a catalogue of scribal styles and estimates of date as discussed in Strugnell (1969–71) and supplemented by Florentino García Martínez's notes in *Literatura judía intertestamentaria*, pp. 96-107, and the carbon 14 test-results.

1. *4QpIsa^a (4Q161)*: rustic semiformal; same scribe or school that copied 4Q166 and 4Q171; developed Herodian (c. 20–70 CE).
2. *4QpIsa^b (4Q162)*: vulgar semiformal; defective orthography; before Herodian period (i.e. prior to 30 BCE).
3. *4QpIsa^c (4Q163)*: two scribes of the Hasmonean semiformal style, one hand being more cursive than the other; oldest copy of pesharim (c. 100 BCE); same scribal tradition as 1QS.
4. *4QpIsa^d (4Q164)*: semicursive Hasmonean; early Herodian (c. 30 BCE to 20 CE).
5. *4QpIsa^e (4Q165)*: formal hand; early Herodian (c. 30 BCE to 20 CE).
6. *4QpHos^a (4Q166)*: rustic semiformal; developed Herodian (c. 20–70 CE); cf. 4Q171 and 4Q161.
7. *4QpHos^b (4Q167)*: rustic semiformal; slightly earlier than the script of 4Q166 (c. 20-70 CE).
8. *1QpMic (1Q14)*: García Martínez (p. 99) suggested that the copying date is before the first century BCE.
9. *4QpNah (4Q169)*: formal hand; end of Hasmonean or beginning of Herodian periods (c. 60–30 BCE).
10. *1QpHab*: two scribes of the Herodian period (c. 30–1 BCE). AMS: 104–43 BCE and 153–143 BCE (3%) or 120–5 BCE (97%).

11. *1QpZeph (1Q15)*: a single fragment impossible to date.
12. *4QpZeph (4Q170)*: remains are too fragmentary to be dated, though Strugnell noted that this is a rustic, semiformal hand distinct from the usual hand of the pesharim.
13. *1QpPs (1Q16)*: García Martínez (p. 105) dated this text to before the first century BCE.
14. *4QpPs^a (4Q171)*: same hand or school as 4Q161 and 4Q166 (c. 20–70 CE). AMS dates: 22–78 CE and 5–111 CE.
15. *4QpPs^b (4Q173)*: early Herodian (c. 30 BCE to 20 CE); fragment 5 half a century later (c. 20–70 CE).

Information about the dates of the thematic pesharim and other related text is also incomplete:

1. *1QWords of Moses (1Q22)*: before first century BCE
2. *1QLiturgical Text? (1Q30)*: not known
3. *4QOrd^{a, b} (4Q159)*: early Herodian (c. 30–1 BCE), formal hand strongly resembling the writing of 4Q174.
4. *4QFlor (4Q174)*: early Herodian (c. 30–1 BCE) similar hand to 4Q159.
5. *4QCatena^a (4Q177)*: early Herodian (c. 30–1 BCE), rustic semi-formal style.
6. *4QAgesCreat^a (4Q180)*: late Herodian (c. 20–70 CE), formal hand.
7. *4QCommentary on Genesis^a (4Q252)*: early Herodian, formal hand.
8. *CD 4.14 (4Q266 fr. 3.1.7)*: CD is a mediaeval copy.
9. *4QExposition on the Patriarchs (4Q464)*: formal hand of the Herodian period.
10. *11QMelch (11Q13)*: middle of first century BCE.

10. Bibliographical Note

The principal edition of the Habakkuk Pesher is found in the 1950 publication of *The Dead Sea Scrolls of St Mark's Monastery, Volume I* edited by Millar Burrows, John C. Trever and William H. Brownlee. There is a number of subsequent editions, including another by Brownlee (1979) and Maurya P. Horgan (1979). Horgan's book, *Pesharim*, not only provides fresh transcription, translation and commentary of the Habakkuk Pesher, but also the revised editions of all texts considered under the genre of continuous pesharim, incorporating as it does the corrections and alternative readings suggested by John Strugnell (1969–71) in his 113-page review of the *editio princeps* of John Allegro's *Qumran Cave 4. I (4Q158–4Q186)* (1968). On

4Q166–167, there may be some confusion as to their corresponding sigla. In preliminary publications, Allegro referred to 4Q167 as 4QpHos[a] and 4Q166 as 4QpHos[b], but reversed these to the present order when he published the principal edition. Studies prior to 1968, therefore, may reflect the earlier designation of the Hosea pesharim. George J. Brooke and Moshe Bernstein are presently re-editing DJD, 5.

George J. Brooke has re-edited and studied 4Q174 (Brooke 1985) and more recently Annette Steudel (1994) has argued that 4Q174 is part of an eschatological midrash that also includes 4Q177 and possibly 4Q182, 4Q178 and 4Q183. 11QMelch (11Q13) was published by Adam S. van der Woude in 1965, subsequently revised by him and Marinus de Jonge in 1966, and most recently reworked by Emile Puech in 1987. The principal edition has now appeared in DJD, 23.

Photographs of the texts are found appended to the principal editions. However, images of all the scrolls are found in a microfiche version edited by Emanuel Tov in collaboration with Stephen Pfann (*The Dead Sea Scrolls on Microfiche*, 1993) and a digitized version, utilizing computer technology, is available on CD-ROM disk edited by Timothy H. Lim in consultation with Philip S. Alexander (*The Dead Sea Scrolls Electronic Reference Library Volume 1*, 1997). A second volume of *The Dead Sea Scrolls Electronic Reference Library* (1999), with a database edited by E. Tov has now appeared.

A facing Hebrew–German edition of 1QpHab, 4QpNah 4QpPs[a], and 11QMelch was published with masoretic pointing by Eduard Lohse in 1964 (*Die Texte aus Qumran*). Recently Florentino García Martínez and Eibert J.C. Tigchelaar have provided a facing Hebrew–English edition that includes all the texts under discussion here (*The Dead Sea Scrolls Study Edition. I. (1Q1–4Q273). II (4Q274–11Q31)* [1997, 1998]). The standard English translation of the Dead Sea Scrolls remains that of Geza Vermes, now in its fifth and 'complete' edition (*The Complete Dead Sea Scrolls in English* [1997]). Notable, too, are the two English editions of Florentino García Martínez's *The Dead Sea Scrolls Translated: The Qumran Texts in English* (1994 and 1995) which was translated from the Spanish original, and Michael Wise, Martin Abegg and Ed Cook's *The Dead Sea Scrolls: A New Translation* (1996).

Finally, a useful aid for study can be found in Michael Knibb's *The Qumran Community* (1987). While this edition is limited to selected texts and is badly in need of updating, it is characterized by an idiomatic English translation and a careful and balanced commentary.

Unless noted otherwise, the English translation used here will be that of Geza Vermes, *The Complete Dead Sea Scrolls in English*, but the editions and some of the more literal renderings of the continuous pesharim and other sectarian text will be those of Maurya Horgan, *Pesharim* and Michael Knibb, *The Qumran Community*.

2

THE CONTINUOUS PESHARIM

The hermeneutics of Qumran scriptural exegesis are often characterized by scholars as 'fulfilment interpretation'. By this is meant that members of the Qumran community believed that the ancient oracles foretold events that were taking place in their own time. They regarded biblical prophecies to be predictive rather than admonitory. They stood squarely on the confessional stance. Contemporary debates in scholarship about biblical story versus history would have been lost on the Qumran sectarians. They supposed that the prophets, whether Isaiah, Habakkuk or David, were historical figures who lived before them and to whom God had revealed his divine will. This is evident when the pesherist wrote: 'God told (*yedaver*) Habakkuk to write that which would happen to the final generation' (1QpHab 7.1-2).

But this prophetic revelation was only partial, since the Qumran community also believed in a form of continuous revelation. While members of the community maintained that God had revealed himself to Habakkuk, the seventh-century prophet saw, as it were, only in part. What the pesherist believed was that Habakkuk did not understand and could not have understood that the words of his own prophecy prefigured events that were to be fulfilled some six centuries later: 'but He [i.e. God] did not make known to him [i.e. Habakkuk] when time would come to an end' (1QpHab 7.2).

Of course the pesherist would not have enumerated time in centuries as is done today. He could have followed a reckoning of time by the 364-day calendar or by a cycle of Jubilee years or simply thought of Habakkuk as a prophet of the distant past. Whatever method of calculation he used, it is true to say that the chronological posture is that of viewing events in the pesherist's own time as having been foretold by the oracles of the past.

The partial and subsequent revelations are eloquently articulated by the pesherist when he commented on ch. 2, vv. 1-2 of Habakkuk's prophecy (1QpHab 6.15–7.6). Note how the Lord's answer is interpreted.

I will take my stand to watch and will station myself upon my fortress. I will
watch to see what He will say to me and how [He will answer] my complaint.
And the Lord answered [and said to me, 'Write down the vision and make it
plain] upon the tablets, that [he who reads] may read it speedily (Hab. 2.1-2) [ ].
And God told Habakkuk to write down that which would happen to the final
generation, but He did not make known to him when time would come to an
end. And as for that which He said, *That he who reads it may read it speedily*
(Hab. 2.2): interpreted this concerns the Teacher of Righteousness, to whom
God made known all the mysteries of the words of His servants the Prophets
(ll. 1-2).

It is widely held that the oracles of Habakkuk originated from different
circumstances and were subsequently put together by editors as evidenced
by some awkward transitions between sections and the inclusion of the
prayer of the third chapter in the *Odes* of the LXX. In their redacted form,
the first two chapters of the prophecy begin with a conventional enough
complaint by the prophet in seeking vindication of divine providence in the
presence of evil. The theme of theodicy is, of course, not distinctive as it is
found in other prophetic and wisdom literature. It is the solution to the first
complaint that marks out Habakkuk's oracles, for Yahweh's answer to the
presence of wickedness within Judah is to rouse her fierce enemies, the
Chaldeans, who according to the prophet is evil and merciless. From v. 12,
ch. 1 onwards, attention is shifted from the wickedness within Judah to the
Chaldeans as the prophet wrestles with the reality that the solution is worse
than the problem.

The two chapters can be divided into the following: superscription (1.1);
first complaint about why the wicked within Judah continue to flourish
(1.2-4); Yahweh's answer in rousing the fierce and violent Chaldeans (often
identified with the neo-Babylonians) for judgment (1.5-11); the prophet's
astonishment that God should not just tolerate this evil, foreign nation but
use them as divine instruments (1.12-17); Yahweh's second answer is to ask
Habakkuk to wait patiently for another vision and record it plainly on tablets
(2.1-4); followed by five woes against the Chaldeans who are arrogant in
amassing wealth that do not belong to them and in plundering nations (2.5-
8), profiting by evil gain (2.9-11), building a town by bloodshed and iniquity
(2.12-14), making their neighbours drunk (2.15-17), and worshipping useless
idols (2.18-20).

In the above gobbet, God instructed Habakkuk to record plainly on
wooden tablets Yahweh's answer to the prophet's second complaint about
why divine judgment is being brought about by the enemies of Judah, the
Chaldeans (Hab. 1.12-17). Earlier, the prophet had grumbled at divine
inaction in allowing the wicked within Judah to oppress the righteous (Hab.
1.2-5); he sought vindication in the ways of the divine amid evil. As an
answer Yahweh assured Habakkuk that there is yet another 'vision' (*hazon*)

concerning the 'appointed time' (*mo'ed*) and 'end-time' (*qets*). Habakkuk should infer from this that God will indeed fulfil this subsequent prophecy. If this 'vision' tarries or is delayed, then the prophet should wait patiently, because it will come timeously, although precisely when has not been specified by the answer.

Writing several centuries later (c. 50 BCE), the Qumran pesherist took his cue from the manifold vision of Habakkuk and interpreted the subsequent biblical verses (Hab. 2.3-20) as the verbal expression of the promised vision that was once written on those wooden tablets (*'for there shall be yet another vision concerning the appointed time'*, Hab. 2.3 in 1QpHab 7.5). Modern scholars of the prophecy usually dissect Hab. 2.6-20 into five separate 'woes' distinct from the first five verses of ch. 2, but the Qumran commentator read the whole as belonging to the same revealed vision. Thus, Hab. 2.5-6 are cited and interpreted together in 1QpHab 8.3-13.

According to the Qumran sectarian, God did reveal to Habakkuk that which would happen in the final generation. What was withheld from him was the precise moment of the end-time and the specific historical references of his prophecy. By interpreting the biblical text in relation to his own situation, the pesherist was asserting that he knew what Habakkuk did not know, that the prophecies were beginning to be fulfilled in his lifetime, and that the end-time was drawing nigh. He knew more than Habakkuk, but he too was awaiting the final end-time. As has been discussed recently by Annette Steudel (1994: 161-69, 187-89 and 1992: 539-40), the Habakkuk pesherist lived through the predicted, but unfulfilled, end-time. Thus, he too, like the author of Luke-Acts had to account for the problem of a 'delayed parousia': the unfulfilled expectation of the final end-time and the consequent problems of dashed hopes. To the assurance that the vision testifies truly to the end-time in Hab. 2.3a, the pesherist commented 'this means that the final age shall be prolonged' (1QpHab 7.7-8), and for the apparent delay of the vision in Hab. 2.3b he admonished the men of truth, who continue to observe the law, that the appointed end will indeed come as God has determined it in the mysteries of his wisdom (1QpHab 7.10-14).

Another important hermeneutical principle signalled in the above passage is the vital role of the Teacher of Righteousness. This sacerdotal figure, known in the pesharim and the Damascus Document only by his title, which can equally be translated as 'the righteous teacher', has a unique role in discerning the divine will. To the phrase *'that he who reads may read it speedily'*, which in Hab. 2.2 refers either to the recording of the vision plainly on wooden tablets for all to see or to the legally observant life, the sectarian commentator stated: 'interpreted (*lipšor*) this concerns the Teacher of Righteousness to whom God had made known all the mysteries of (*razey*) His servants the prophets'. The biblical prophecies were couched in mystery (*raz*) and it is the Teacher of

Righteousness who will reveal this mystery. He is identified with the one who reads Habakkuk's wooden tablets easily. He is able to do so, because in his heart 'God (had) set [understanding] that he might interpret all the words of His servants the Prophets' (1QpHab 2.8-9).

The term translated as 'interpreted' is *pišro*, literally 'its [i.e. the verse's or matter's] interpretation *(pesher)*'. It is, of course, the technical term that gives the sectarian interpretation its name and is based upon the semitic root *pšr*, attested in Akkadian, Aramaic, Hebrew and Arabic and meaning 'to loosen, to release and to interpret'. It occurs only once in the Hebrew Bible at Qoh. 8.1 ('Who is like the wise man? And who knows the interpretation [*pešer*] of a thing?') and several times in the Aramaic section of Daniel, ch. 5 vv. 26-28 being the most significant as they interpret the text of an inscription, and not just a vision. It is also related to the use of *ptr*, the more common root in the Hebrew Bible for expressing 'to interpret' and the term used in Joseph's dream interpretations in Genesis 40 and 41.

The sectarian commentator of 1QpHab used the technical term *pesher* to identify 'the reader' of Hab. 2.2 to be the Teacher of Righteousness. He learned this technique of scriptural exegesis from the self-same Teacher, whom, in another passage, he described as having been divinely ordained to interpret *(lipšor)* all the words of the biblical prophets (1QpHab 2.8-10). The infinitive 'to interpret' *(lipšor)*, of course, is derived from the same root as *pesher*. The use of identical terminology suggests that the Teacher of Righteousness adopted a method of scriptural interpretation, inspired by the biblical texts themselves, and many in the Qumran community followed his method in composing what are known today as *pesharim*.

1. Diversity of Exegeses in the Pesharim

In recent years, there has been a growing recognition that pesherite exegesis is in fact more diverse than that which has been described above (Lim 2000b: 63; Bernstein 1994: 69-70). The Habakkuk pesher represents one kind of scriptural interpretation, if an exemplary one, but it would be wrong to assume that this type of exegesis is representative of all the pesharim. In fact, as will be shown below, even within this pesher *par exemple* a range of exegeses is preserved.

1.1 Isaiah
The five pesharim to Isaiah (4Q162-165) were copied by scribes for more than 150 years (c. 100 BCE to 70 CE). The biblical passages quoted are derived from what modern scholarship calls Isaiah (chs. 1–39) and Deutero-Isaiah (chs. 40–55), though there is no evidence that the pesherists made such a distinction. In 3QpIsa (3Q4), a text that does not preserve the

technical term 'pesher', despite its sigla, the commentary begins with the
superscription of the book: 'The vision of Isaiah, the son of A[moz]'.

1.1.1. 4QpIsa^a (4Q161)

The ten preserved fragments of this text have been reconstructed by John
Allegro, John Strugnell and Maurya Horgan into three columns, interpreting
the Assyrian threat against Israel and portrayal of a messianic golden age
(Isa. 10.22–11.5). Much of the commentary has been mutilated, but it is
evident that the pesherist interpreted this portion of Isaiah eschatologically
('as regard the end of days' frags. 2-6, col. 2.26). In several places there are
references to 'the Kittim' (frags. 7-10 col. 3.7, 9?, 10 and 12) which, in the
pesharim, are to be read as a coded reference to the Romans (see Chapter 5).
The original context has now been lost, but there appears to have been
envisioned a 'battle of the Kittim' (frags. 7-10, col. 3.11). The leader of this
eschatological battle was a figure known as 'the Prince of the Congregation',
who is mentioned in frags. 2-6, col. 2.19 and elsewhere in the Qumran
scrolls. He seems to have been identified messianically with '[the scion of]
David' (frags. 7-10, col. 3.22). There is also a reference to 'one of the priest
of repute' (frags. 7-10, col. 3.29). This Isaiah pesher has several affinities
with *Sefer Ha-Milhamah* (4Q285), better known by its misleading title as
'the slain messiah' text, and the *Rule of the Congregation* (1QSa), both in the
way that they have used Isaiah 10–11 as prooftext and also the figures who
appear in their exposition.

Because of its fragmentary state, the nature of its commentary cannot be
ascertained with confidence. Like other pesharim, it appears to quote a biblical
lemma, followed by an introductory formula and comment. It also appears to
re-cite a biblical text (namely Isa. 11.3b in col. 3.27) as is commonly done in
other pesharim, Characteristic of this and three other pesharim (4Q162-163
and 4Q165) is the relatively longer proportion of biblical quotation to
comment. The use of an empty line (frags. 2-6.2.20 and frags. 7-10.3.14, 21)
and a space to separate the lemma from the comment (frags. 2-6.2.10) are
exegetical scribal practices also found in 4Q166 and 4Q167.

1.1.2. 4QpIsa^b (4Q162)

The single fragment of three columns of this pesher interprets Isa. 5.5-14, 24-
25, 29-30 and possibly 6.9. The biblical text appears to have been exegeted
eschatologically ('as regards the end of days', col. 2.1). But the commentary is
brief and seems to be no more than mere glosses. The 'scoffers' in Jerusalem,
possibly a coded reference to the followers of the Wicked Priest, being
identified with the pleasure seekers of Isa. 5.11-14 who neglect the deeds of
Yahweh (col. 2.6-7).

1.1.3. 4QpIsaᶜ (4Q163)

The oldest copy of the Isaiah pesharim, 4Q163, is palaeographically dated to c. 100 BCE. The 61 fragments of this scroll are written exceptionally on papyrus rather than on skin. The reconstruction into columns by the editors is tentative.

According to Horgan's edition, the pesher would have quoted passages from 22 chapters of Isaiah (chs. 8–30). If this is correct, then one has to assume that in its original form, the pesher would have to have been very long indeed. Like the other Isaiah pesharim, in 4QpIsaᶜ the ratio of quoted biblical text to commentary is large. Unusually, this pesher appears to also have quoted from other biblical texts: some unidentified passage in Jeremiah (frag. 1.4), Zech 11.11 (frag. 21.7), and possibly Hos. 6.9a (frag. 23, col. 2.14).

1.1.4. 4QpIsaᵈ (4Q164)

The three fragments of this scroll preserve an eschatological interpretation of the post-exilic passage in Isa. 54.11-12 about the rebuilding of the new Jerusalem. Significantly, the laying of her foundations with precious stones is related to the hierarchical structure of the community as reflected in the Rule of Community (1QS).

> *And I will lay your foundations with sapphires* (Isa. 54.11c). Interpreted this concerns the Priests and the people who laid the foundations of the Council of the Community…the congregation of His elect (shall sparkle) like a sapphire among stones…[*And I will make*] *all your pinnacles* [*of agate*] (Isa. 54.12a). Interpreted, this concerns the twelve [chief Priests] who shall enlighten by judgement of the Urim and Thumim.. which are absent from them, like the sun will all its light, and like the moon…[*And all your gates of carbuncles*] (Isa. 54.12b). Interpreted, this concerns the chiefs of the tribes of Israel…

The preserved proportion of biblical text to commentary is shorter than the rest of the Isaiah pesharim. The commentary does not simply gloss over the biblical texts as in other Isaiah pesharim.

1.1.5. 4QpIsaᵉ (4Q165)

Eleven fragments have been assembled together as part of the fifth pesher to Isaiah. As they are presented in DJD, 5, pl. IX, the biblical verses would have been in some disorder: frags. 1-2 quote from Isa. 40.11-12; frag. 3 from Isa. 14.19; frag. 4 Isa. 15.4-5; frag. 5 from Isa. 21.10-15; frag. 6 from Isa. 32.5 and 32.6-7 and frag. 11 from Isa. 11.11-12a. Perhaps they should be rearranged according to the MT order. There is not much that is preserved in the commentary that is found in between long quotations from the biblical text. There are tantalizing references to 'poor one[s]' (frag. 7.2) and 'men of the commun[ity]' (frag. 9.3).

1.2. Hosea

The two pesharim to Hosea were copied in the Herodian period (c. 30 BCE–
70 CE), with 4Q167 slightly earlier. Strugnell suggested that the numerous
fragments of 4Q167 may have originally belonged to one pesher on several
minor prophets (1969–71: 199 and 204). If true, then 4QpHos^b would have
been a very large scroll.

1.2.1. 4QpHos^a (4Q166)

The one large fragment of this pesher interprets the biblical text of Hos. 2.8-
14 which concern Yahweh's response to the unfaithfulness of his whore-wife,
Israel. Although the commentary is not specific enough, Dupont-Sommer
(1970–71: 413) and Amoussine (1969–71: 547) believe that this pesher refers
to the period immediately before the Romans' settlement of Palestine in 63
BCE. According to this view, the mention of 'famine' in col. 2.12 denotes the
drought mentioned by Josephus in the *Antiquities*. Dupont-Sommer's further
suggestion that 'the nations' (col. 2.13) is a reference to the Romans is
correctly rejected on the grounds that one would have expected 'Kittim'. But
other suggested references to 'the nations' (as Seleucids or the Nabatean
troops) are equally speculative. Blank lines are evident at col. 1.13-14 and col.
2.7 and lemma/comment spaces in col. 2.6 and 11.

1.2.2. 4QpHos^b (4Q167)

The 38 fragments of this pesher preserve the interpretation of verses from
three chapters of Hosea (5, 6 and 8). Tantalizingly in this badly mutilated text
are references to: 'the lion of wrath' (frag. 2.2) who in 4QpNah 3-4.1.5-5
appears to be a coded reference to Alexander Jannaeus 'who hangs men alive';
'Ephraim' (frag. 2.3), the eponymous name of Joseph's son, who in 4QpNah
(frags. 3-4.1.12; frags. 3-4.2.2, 8; frags. 3-4.3.5) and 4QpPs^a (frags. 1-10.2.18)
most likely denotes the opponents of the sect, the Pharisees. Horgan (1979:
150) sees in the phrase 'their teacher' (frags. 5-6.2) a possible reference to the
Teacher of Righteousness, but this may originally have been an exegesis of
yoreh in Hos. 6.3 which refers to the downpour of the rain. She also suggests
that 'and that' (frags. 10, 26.1) is exceptionally used here as an introductory,
rather than a re-citation, formula (Horgan 1979: 149), but *ašer* here may well
be part of the biblical text of Hos. 6.9 and a variant of *ky* (Lim 1997a: 80).
Both line-spaces and lemma/comment spaces may also have been used in frag.
4, line 3, frag. 7, line 3 and frag. 8, line 2, and frag. 13, line 8.

1.3. Micah

1.3.1. 1QpMic (4Q14)

The 23 fragments of this badly mutilated pesher preserve interpretations of
verses from Micah 1 and 6. The arrangment of the fragments is uncertain and

there is very little commentary that has survived the ravages of time. There are, nevertheless, several possible sectarian references in frag. 10 to 'the Tea[ch]er of Righteousness' (line 4), 'the chosen ones' (line 5) and 'the council of the community' (line 6). The tetragram is written in palaeo-Hebrew letters (frags. 1-5.1), but its significance as an indicator of the non-authoritative status of a document is now questioned, given that the practice also occurs in 'biblical texts'.

1.4. Nahum
1.4.1. 4QpNah (4Q169)
The five fragments of 4Q169 interpret passages from all three chapters of the prophecy of Nahum. One of the most important pesharim, 4QpNah is sometimes described as 'the historical pesher', because on two occasions it appears to drop its cloak of coded references to mention explicitly the names of '[Deme]trius' and 'Antiochus':

> *Where the lion went to enter the lion's cub and [no one to disturb* (Nah. 2.12). The interpretation of it concerns Deme]trius, King of Greece, who sought to enter Jerusalem on the advice of the Seekers-After-Smooth-Things, [but God did not give Jerusalem] into the power of the kings of Greece from Antiochus until the rise of the rulers of the Kittim' (frags. 3-4, col. 1.1-3).

'The lion' of Nah. 2.12 is interpreted as a prophetic reference to 'Demetrius, King of Greece', whom most scholars identify with the Seleucid ruler of Damascus, Demetrius III Eucareus (95–88 BCE). The events referred to here are thought to correspond to Josephus's account in *Antiquities* 13.372-83 and *War* 1.90-8 which describe the rebellion of Jews against their High Priest and ruler, Alexander Jannaeus (103–76 BCE). The rebels, led by the Pharisees, sought the help of Demetrius in overthrowing Alexander, but at the prospect of foreign Seleucid rule opposition galvanized and the rebellious Jews switched sides and fell into coalition with the High Priest. Those called 'the Seekers-After-Smooth-Things', therefore, are to be identified with the Pharisees who had enlisted the help of Demetrius and 800 of whom Alexander subsequently crucified ('he [i.e. Alexander] would hang men up alive', frags. 3-4, col. 1.7-8; Josephus, *War* 1.97). The epithet of 'the Seeker-After-Smooth-Things' is a translation of the Hebrew *dorshey ha-halaqot* which, as Lawrence Schiffman (1993) has emphasized, is a disparaging pun on *halakha*, the technical term for Jewish law in rabbinic literature. These 'Seekers-After-Smooth-Things', likely a polemical reference to the apparently pharisaic penchant to find 'the smooth things' (cf. Isa. 30.10), are further identified eschatologically with 'the city of Ephraim...at the end of days' (frags. 3-4, col. 2.2).

According to the Nahum pesherist, Demetrius sought to enter Jerusalem. Although the text is mutilated at this crucial point, the reconstruction 'but

God did not give Jerusalem' is widely accepted in light of the fact that Demetrius entered but did not take the Holy City. If this is correct, then it appears that the pesherist saw the hand of God at work in preserving Jerusalem from foreign control. This entire period, the pesherist encapsulated in the phrase as 'from (using the Hebrew *myn* exceptionally in a temporal sense) Antiochus to the rise of the rulers of the Kittim', that is from Antiochus Epiphanes (175–164 BCE) to the Roman settlement of Palestine in 63 BCE.

Other groups are also mentioned in the pesher: 'the simple ones of Ephraim' are the legally naïve who, according to the pesherist, are led astray by the Pharisees; 'Manasseh', the great and honoured ones (frags. 3-4.3.9), appears to be an allusion to the Sadducees; 'Judah' denotes the Qumran community (frags. 3-4.3.4); and the 'Kittim' is found in its usual designation as the Romans. There is also a reference to 'the House of Peleg' (frags. 3-4.4.1), which Richard White (1990) has identified with those who separated from Jerusalem cult and built a Temple at Leontopolis.

The nature of this pesher's biblical interpretation calls for comment. First, there is a conscious use of spacing to distinguish biblical lemma from commentary (frags. 3-4.1.6, 9; 2.1, 10; 3.2, 8; 4.5) as in 4QpIsa[a] and 4QpHos[a,b]. Secondly, there is a higher proportion of what is sometimes inappropriately called 'atomization'. A better way of describing this phenomenon, which is not a reduction to particles or elements, is the segmentation and singling out of words or short phrases of the biblical text for comment. Thus, for instance, 'his prey' of Nah. 2.14 (frags. 3-4.1.9) is quoted again in line 11 and epexegetically explained as a reference to 'the wealth that the [prie]sts of Jerusalem have amas[sed]'. The difference between this method of segmentation and that of re-citation is one of degree, not kind.

Thirdly, the pesherist understands some of the words of the lemma to be polysemic and his comments as part of an internal discourse with the biblical text. In Nah. 2.1–3.19, what is often called 'the Oracles against Nineveh', the reference to 'lions' and 'young lions' is an allusion to the strength of Assyria, symbols that recall the depiction of this most powerful of mammals on reliefs. As discussed above, the pesherist identified 'the lion' of Nah. 2.12 to be Demetrius (frags. 3-4.1.1-3). This same lion is then equated for a second time with 'the young lion of wrath who hangs men alive' (lines 4-7), namely Alexander Jannaeus. Moreover, 'the young lions' of Nah. 2.14 are said to refer to 'his great ones' (lines 10-11). A look at the two Hebrew words for 'lion' and 'young lion' is instructive:

> **lion** (*arî*) (Nah. 2.12-13) = Demetrius (line 2) and 'the young lion (*kephîr*) of wrath' (line 4)
> **your young lions** (*kepîrêkah*) (Nah. 2.14) = 'his (i.e. Alexander's) great ones' (line 10)

The English word 'lion', translating the Hebrew *'arî*, has two meanings for the Nahum pesherist. It refers first to the Seleucid King, Demetrius, and second to 'the young lion of wrath'. The words 'young lion' translate the Hebrew *kephîr*. This same term, moreover, appears in the next verse of Nah. 2.14 as a suffixed plural (*kepîrêkah*) which the pesherist interpreted to be 'his (i.e. the young lion's) great ones'. In other words, the Nahum pesherist understood 'lion' (*'arî*) to have had two referents, and used the word of a subsequent biblical verse for 'young lion', *kephîr*, in his interpretation of one of them.

Finally, the mixing of historical and symbolic references in the commentary is an imitation of the prophetic oracles of Nahum where references to the city of Nineveh lie side by side with the figurative depiction of Assyria as 'lions'.

1.5. Habakkuk

1.5.1. 1QpHab

Several features of the Habakkuk pesher have already been discussed above and others, for instance the personalities of the Wicked Priest, Teacher of Righteousness, the Liar and the Kittim, will be treated elsewhere. Here, the discussion focuses on the structure of the commentary.

Exegetical Structure

The Habakkuk pesherist dissected his biblical text in the following way. Table 2.1 shows the correspondence between the prophecy of Habakkuk and the commentary where they are preserved.

Table 2.1

1QpHab	Sectarian Comment	Habakkuk	Content
1.1-3	Eschatological orientation?	1.1-2a	Superscript (1.1) and beginning of first complaint (1.2a)
1.4-5	Mention of 'crying out' against violence	[1.2b]	
1.5-6	Mention of 'God', 'oppression' and 'unfaithfulness'	1.3a	
1.7-10	Mention of 'strife' and 'quarrel'	[1.3b]	
1.10-11	Rejection of the law of God	1.4a	
1.12-14	Teacher of Righteousness against [the liar]	1.4b	
1.14-16	Mutilated	1.4b	
1.16–2.10	Special role of the Teacher of Righteousness, the treachery of the traitors/nations and Liar.	1.5	Yahweh's response

1QpHab	Sectarian Comment	Habakkuk	Content
2.10-16	Chaldeans identified with swift and battle-ready Kittim	1.6a	
2.16–3.2	Kittim's devastation	1.6b	
3.2-6	All nations' fear and dread of the Kittim	1.6b-7	
3.6-14	Military might of the Kittim	1.8-9a	
3.14-	Mutilated	1.9a-9b	
4.1-3	Kittim's scorn of kings and princes	1.10a	
4.3-9	Rulers of the Kittim and their sieges	1.10b	
4.9-13	Guilty house of Kittim and the succession of their rulers	1.11a	
4.13-	Mutilated	1.11b	
5.1-6	Assurance of God's faithfulness for his people and promise of judgment against the wicked	1.12b-13a	second complaint
5.6-8	The purity of those who have kept God's commandments	1.13a	
5.8-12	The silence of the House of Absalom and the confrontation between the Teacher of Righteousness and the Liar	1.13b	
5.12–6.2	The plunder and wealth of the Kittim	1.14-16	
6.2-5	Kittim sacrifice to their standards	1.16a	
6.5-8	forced tribute imposed by the Kittim on many people	1.16b	
6.8-12	Ruthlessness of the Kittim in killing young and old.	1.17	
6.12–7.2	Habakkuk's prophecy fulfilled at the end-time	2.1-2	Yahweh's response and announcement of another vision to come
7.3-5	God's revelation to the Teacher of Righteousness	2.2b	
7.5-8	Delayed end-time will be greater than what the prophets have said	2.3a	
7.9-14	Men of truth will not slacken in their observance of the law	2.3b	
7.14-16	Mention of 'doubling over' and 'judgment'	2.4a	
[7.17]-8.3	God will save those who observe the law and are faithful to the Teacher of Righteousness	2.4b	
8.3-13	The Wicked Priest who became arrogant, greedy and debauched	2.5-6	First Woe
8.13–9.3	The priest who rebelled inflicted with evil diseases	2.7-8a	

1QpHab	Sectarian Comment	Habakkuk	Content
9.3–7	The last priests of Jerusalem who amass wealth will be handed over to the army of the Kittim	2.8a	
9.8-12	The Wicked Priest was handed over to his enemies because of the wrong done to the Teacher of Righteousness and God's chosen ones	2.8b	
9.12-10.2	Mention of illegitimate building	2.9-11	Second woe
10.2-5	Eschatological house of judgment	2.10b	
10.5-13	The Liar's illicit building of a city of vanity	2.12-13	Third woe
10.14-11.2	The revelation of knowledge in the end time will be as abundant as the waters of the sea	2.14	
11.2-8	The Wicked Priest's pursuit of the Teacher of Righteousness to his place of exile on the Day of Atonement	2.15	Fourth woe
11.8-[16]	The priest who was consumed by his own drink	2.16	
12.1-6	The Wicked Priest's punishment for acting wickedly against the community	2.17a	
12.6-10	Jerusalem and sanctuary defiled by the Wicked Priest	2.17b	
12.10-14	Impotence of idols	2.18	Fifth woe
12.14-13.4	Eschatological judgment on the nations that serve stone and wood	2.19-20	

It is a truism to say that the pesherist did not read the prophecy of Habakkuk as modern scholars do today. The ancient reading of these oracles was not founded upon a critical approach. It is revelatory and inspired exegesis, but one that has some structure to it.

To begin with, it is important to note how the Table 2.1 differs from almost all editions and translations. In this table, the Wicked Priest does not appear until col. 8, whereas he is commonly reconstructed to be opposing the Teacher of Righteousness in col. 1. But this reconstruction is questionable (for full details see Lim 2001a: 47-50; and independently suggested by Bernstein 2000: 650).

The reconstructed line 13 of col. 1 of 1QpHab reads: '[Its interpretation: the *wicked* is the Wicked Priest]'. This is a comment on the partially extant verse of Hab. 1.4b: '[*For the wicked surrou*]*nd the righteous*' (line 12). Line 13 also partially preserves the phrase: '[*the righteous*] is the Teacher of Righteousness'. The reconstruction of 'the righteous' and 'the wicked' with the Teacher of Righteousness and Wicked Priest respectively is based upon the interpretation of another biblical passage (Ps. 37.32-33) in a different pesher

(4QpPs[a] frags. 1-10, col. 4.7-10). It is to be doubted whether the Habakkuk pesherist would likewise interpret his biblical material. In 1QpHab 5.8-12, which interprets Hab. 1.13, the 'righteous one' of the biblical lemma is identified with the Teacher of Righteousness, but 'a wicked one' with the Liar and not the Wicked Priest. In other words, in the only other place where the biblical lemma attests to the adjective 'wicked', the identification is with the Liar. Given that the Liar is prominent a few lines later at the beginning of col. 2 and that the next reference to the Wicked Priest does not occur until ch. 8, then it is preferable to reconstruct line 13 as a reference to the Liar and not the Wicked Priest: 'Its interpretation: '[*the wicked* is the man of the lie and *the righteous*] is the Teacher of Righteousness'.

Reading the text this way, it appears that there is some discernible structure to the Habakkuk pesher. The Wicked Priest appears for the first time in col. 8 at the point where the biblical prophecy begins a series of five woes. As already mentioned above, the citation of the lemma in col. 8.3-8 blurs the distinction between vv. 5 and 6 of ch. 2. Moreover, not all the 'woes' are understood as references to the Wicked Priest. The third woe concerns the Liar and his illicit building activity in Jerusalem and the fifth woe is about the idolatry of the nations. Nevertheless, the Wicked Priest does appear only in the woe section of Habakkuk's prophecy.

Another interesting feature about the structure is the centrality of vv. 1-5 of ch. 2 for the prophet and pesherist alike. In the prophecy, Yahweh's answer to the second complaint is the crux of Habakkuk's message in the first two chapters. The divine declaration that there is yet another vision to come acts as an assurance of future reprieve for those who presently fear and suffer from the Chaldeans. For the pesherist, the whole pericope, from the writing down of the vision on tablets, to the ease by which one can read it, to the promise of another vision, to the righteous man who lives by his faithfulness, serves as the main focus of exposition on his hermeneutical process of reading and interpreting ancient oracles. True, col. 2.8-10, also underscore the chosen role of the Teacher of Righteousness in the interpretative act, but this passage is secondary to its main concern with the Liar and the traitors.

Finally, apart from the passing reference in 1QpHab 9.7, the Kittim or Romans (see Chapter 5) occur only in those passages of the biblical text where the Chaldeans are in view. The first mention of the Kittim occurs precisely with the verse that declares '*For behold I am raising up the Chaldeans, that bitter [and ha]sty nation*' (Hab. 1.6; 1QpHab 2.10-15). The last explicit reference to them occurs in the middle of col. 6 and its exegesis of Hab 1.17. Note that 'the nations' (*ha-goyim*) condemned for idolatry at the end of cols. 12 and 13 are not the Kittim as such, despite the equation of 'nation' (*ha-goy*) in Hab. 1.6a with the Kittim in col. 2.12. This is a phenomenon, discussed above, that uses the same term to designate different referents.

Other Features. The inherent exegesis of the Habakkuk pesher is the primary reason for its prominence in discussions about the genre. Every feature, barring the explicit historical reference in 4QpNah, ascribed to the pesharim generally can be found here: eschatological orientation (e.g. judgment in the end time, col. 10.2-5; col. 12.12–13.4), segmentation (e.g. 'Lebanon', 'beasts', col. 12.3-4), re-citation (e.g. 'and when it says', col. 2.2b), contemporization of prophecy (e.g. col. 7.1-14), and glosses (e.g. on idolatry, col. 12.12–13.4). There is diversity in this one pesher.

Noteworthy too are scribal techniques that appear in the scroll: spaces are used here as in other pesharim to mark off lemmata from commentary. Following the last word of the commentary in col. 13 is a large blank area, evidently denoting the ending of the pesher. There are curious marks that look like an X which may be part of the cryptic script, but their significance is unclear.

1.6. Zephaniah
The prophecy of Zephaniah is an obvious source for the sectarian critique of the Temple and its cult. The officials and priests of the defiled and soiled city of Chapter 3, a reference to Jerusalem no doubt, are depicted as 'roaring lions' and those who have 'profaned the sacred' (vv. 3-4). It is not surprising, therefore, to find two pesharim to this prophecy. Resonance of these oracles 'in the days of King Josiah' (1.1) would have reverberated in the ears of members of the Qumran community.

1.6.1. 1QpZeph (1Q15)
One fragment of six lines quoting Zeph. 1.18b–2.2, this text is difficult to read (PAM 40.497), because the skin has darkened. If the pieces of the fragment have been correctly reconstructed, then it would appear to have cited Zeph. 1.18b–2.2. There appears to be the beginning of a commentary ('pesher', line 4) after the biblical text. How extensive this commentary was originally cannot now be known The extant biblical lemma appears to have consisted of three verses as compared to just one for 4QpZeph (4Q170). The tetragram is written in palaeo-Hebrew script in lines 3 and 4 and possibly elsewhere.

1.6.2. 4QpZeph (4Q170)
The two tiny fragments of this pesher can be reconstructed as an interpretation of Zeph. 1.12-13a interspersed with comments. The technical term 'pesher' is preserved in line 4 (*pišro*), DJD, 5, pl. XIV.

1.7. Psalms

The Psalms are some of the most beloved Scriptures of the Qumran community as evidenced by the central role that they play in numerous sectarian texts (e.g. 4Q174, 4Q177). There are also some 40 or so Psalms scrolls preserved in the Qumran library and it is possible that they, together with Deuteronomy and Isaiah, are the most numerous of the biblical texts. The three pesharim to Psalms interpret Psalm 68, 37, 45, 60 and 129.

1.7.1. 1QpPs (1Q16)

Of the 18 badly mutilated fragments that belong to this pesher, only three (frags. 3, 8 and 9) preserve identifiable biblical texts (Ps. 68.13, 26b-27a and 30-31) with commentary. The extent of the damage has rendered the interpretation incomprehensible. The technical term, in its typical suffixed form (*pišro*) occurs twice in frag. 9, lines 1 and 4 and the name '[K]ittim' is plausibly restored in line 4 (PAM 40.540).

1.7.2. 4QpPsᵃ (4Q171)

The most substantial of the Psalms commentaries, the ten fragments of this pesher interpret three biblical songs. Psalm 37 is an instructional hymn of encouragement by an elder about the abiding faithfulness of Yahweh amid the presence of wickedness and is ideally suited for the sectarian concerns. Psalm 45 is a royal wedding song whose composer ('[I] ad[dress my song to the king]. And my tongue is the pen of [a skilled scribe]', v. 2b) appears to have been identified with 'the Teacher [of Righteousness]' (frags. 1-10, col. 4.27). Psalm 60 is, according to its superscription, a *miktam* psalm, one of five in the traditional Psalter, that appears to have been originally inscribed on a tablet or wall. Fragment 13 preserves a quotation and interpretation of vv. 8-9, preceded by a vacat or empty line (frags. 1-10, col. 4.22). This does not mean that the interpretation of Psalm 60 began at v. 8. The use of a vacant line is characteristic of this pesher in marking out perceived sense units (so frags. 1-10, col. 2.21; col. 4.6, 22; but not frags. 1-10, col. 2.6 which may have been divided according to the acrostic pattern). Although the text is badly damaged, the mention of 'Manasseh' and 'Ephraim' in vv. 8-9, appears to occasion an interpretative comment now lost (frag. 13).

The pesher of Psalm 37 is well known primarily because it seems to mention an attempt made by the Wicked Priest to take the life of the Teacher of Righteousness. In frags. 1-10, col. 4.7-10, the pesherist cites vv. 32-33 of Psalm 37 which refer to 'a wicked one lying in ambush for the righteous one, [seeking to put him to death]'. Although lacunose, the commentary is often reconstructed so that the identification of 'a wicked one' is made with 'the Wicked Priest' and 'the righteous' with 'the Teacher of Righteousness. Apparently, the pesherist saw in the words of the biblical text a reference to what actually took place in his own time. If the reconstruction is correct, then the Wicked Priest attempted to put the Teacher of Righteousness to death. Moreover, this violent act was provoked 'because he (i.e. the Teacher of Righteousness) had sent the law (*ha-torah*) to him (i.e. the Wicked Priest)'. Some scholars have speculated that 'the law' mentioned here is none other than the Temple Scroll or MMT, and that the incident referred to the time when, mentioned in the Habakkuk Pesher, when the Wicked Priest pursued the Teacher of Righteousness to his 'house of exile' on the Day of Atonement (1QpHab 11.2-8). Neither of these views can be substantiated. Nor is it legitimate to extrapolate the pesherist's method of exegesis to the Habakkuk pesher as mentioned above.

The remaining interpretation of Psalm 37 in 4QpPs[a] includes several figures, known from other pesharim and the Qumran scrolls, to 'the man of the lie' or 'liar' (frag. 1-10, col. 1.26; col. 4.14), 'the congregation of the poor (or poor ones)' (frags. 1-10, col. 2.10; 3.10), 'the ruthless ones of the covenant who are in the house of Judah' (frags. 1-10, col. 2.14), 'the council of the community' (frags. 1-10, col. 2.15), 'Ephraim' and 'Manasseh' (frags. 1-10, col. 2.18), and 'the congregation of the community' (frags. 1-10, col. 4.19; cf. 1QSa 2.21). There is a clear eschatological tone in this pesher and many of the references are unspecific. Even so, the pesherist seems to have been living at a time when there was both external opposition from 'the liar', 'Ephraim and Manasseh', 'the Wicked priest', as well as internal strife, 'the ruthless ones' within the house of Judah.

Despite the use of empty lines as spacers, the commentary is continuous. Thus, even though line 6 of frags. 1-10, col. 2 is blank, the interpretation of the disappearance of the wicked depends upon the biblical text of Ps. 37.10 cited in both lines 7 and 5.

1.7.3. 4QpPs[b] (4Q173)

As mentioned in Chapter 1, only four of the five fragments of this text belong to a second pesher on the Psalms. Fragment 5 is palaeographically later than the other four fragments and it probably belongs to another exegetical text that quotes Ps. 118.20. Of the fragments of 4QpPs[b], frag. 4 preserves only the biblical text of Ps. 129.7-8, with a few letters possibly from the commentary. Fragment 1, line 4 and frag. 2 line 2 preserve the epithet of 'the Teacher of Righteousness', and line 5 of the former can be reconstructed with a reasonable degree of certainty to read 'the prie]st at the end of ti]me'. Fragment 1, line 6 may have been left empty.

2. Common and Distinctive Features

The genre of sectarian exegesis known as 'the pesher' is a typological construct of Qumran scholarship and as such it correctly identifies common features shared between the 15 texts examined above. These features, however, are not as numerous as is often implied in books, articles and surveys. All the continuous pesharim share only the following: (1) the continuous quotation of sections, large or small, of a biblical text; (2) the use of the technical term 'pesher' in the introductory formula of the interpretation; and (3) the identification of a figure in the biblical text with another, apparently contemporary one. The eschatological orientation is probably also prevalent, although not all of the pesharim have preserved evidence of it (4QpZeph). Other features, for example the segmentation of the biblical text in a re-citation, are found in one or more pesharim, but not in all of them.

The exegetical and thematic affinities between the pesharim can be noted in Tables 2.2 and 2.3.

Table 2.2. Exegetical Methods

Pesher	Exegetical Method	Other Pesharim
4QpIsa[a]	1) Long biblical quotations 2) Line-spacing 3) Lemma/comment spacing 4) Re-citation	1) 4QpIsa[b c e] 2) 4QpHos[a b], 1QpHab, 4QpPs[a b] 3) 4QpHos[a b], 4QpNah, 1QpHab, 4QpPs[a] 4) 4QpNah, 1QpHab, 4QpHos[b], 4QpZeph
4QpIsa[b]	Long biblical quotations	1) 4QpIsa[a c e]
4QpIsa[c]	1) Long biblical quotations 2) Quoting other biblical texts	1) 4QpIsa[a b e] 2) None
4QpIsa[d]	Segmentation	4QpNah, 1QpHab
4QpIsa[e]	Long biblical quotations	4QpIsa[a b c]
4QpHos[a]	1) Line-spacing 2) Lemma/comment spacing	1) 4QpIsa[a], 4QpHos[b], 1QpHab, 4QpPs[a b] 2) 4QpIsa[a], 4QpHos[b], 4QpNah, 1QpHab, 4QpPs[a]
4QpHos[b]	1) Re-citation? 2) Line-spacing	1) 4QpIsa[a], 4QpNah, 1QpHab, 4QZeph 2) 4QpHos[a,] 1QpHab, 4QpPs[a b]
1QpMic	Palaeo-Hebrew for Tetragram	1QpHab, 1QpZeph
4QpNah	1) Lemma/comment spacing 2) Segmentation 3) Polysemy 4) Explicit historical reference	1) 4QpIsa[a], 4QpHos[a b], 1QpHab, 4QpPs[a b] 2) 4QpIsa[d], 1QpHab 3) 1QpHab 4) none

Pesher	Exegetical Method	Other Pesharim
1QpHab	1) Lemma/comment spacing 2) Segmentation 3) Polysemy 4) Re-citation 5) Palaeo-Hebrew for Tetragram 6) Scribal marks	1) 4QpIsaᵃ, 4QpHosᵃᵇ, 4QpNah, 4QpPsᵃ 2) 4QpNah, 4QpIsaᵈ 3) 4QpIsaᵃ, 4QpNah, 4QpZeph 4) 4QpHosᵇ, 4QpIsaᵃ, 4QpNah 5) 1QpMic, 1QpZeph 6) none
1QpZeph	1) Long biblical quotation 2) Palaeo-Hebrew for Tetragram	1) 4QpIsaᵃ ᵇ ᶜ 2) 1QpMic, 1QpHab
4QpZeph	Re-citation?	4QpIsaᵃ, 4QpHosᵇ, 1QpHab
1QpPs	Insufficient information	
4QpPsᵃ	1) Use of line-spaces 2) Lemma/comment spaces	1) 4QpIsaᵃ, 4QpHosᵃᵇ, 1QpHab, 4QpPsᵇ 2) 4QpIsaᵃ, 4QpHosᵃᵇ, 4QpNah, 1QpHab
4QpPsᵇ	Use of line-spaces	4QpIsaᵃ, 4QpHosᵃᵇ, 1QpHab, 4QpPsᵃ

Table 2.3. Thematic content

Pesher	Personalities, events, sobriquets	Other pesharim	Other Qumran texts
4QpIsaᵃ	Kittim, Prince of the Congregation, eschatological battle, priest of repute	1QpHab, 1QpPs	CD, 1QHᵃ, 1QM. 4Q285, 1QSb, 4Q376
4QpIsaᵇ	Scoffers of Jerusalem	1QpHab	CD, 1QHᵃ
4QpIsaᶜ	Too badly mutilated and unspecific		
4QpIsaᵈ	Council of the community, twelve (chief priests)	1QpHab, 4QpPsᵃ	1QS
4QpIsaᵉ	Poor ones, men of the community	1QpHab	
4QpHosᵃ	Nations	1QpHab	
4QpHosᵇ	Lion of wrath, Ephraim	4QpNah, 4QpPsᵃ	
1QpMic	Teacher of Righteousness, council of the community, chosen ones	4QpIsaᵈ, 4QpNah, 1QpHab, 4QpPsᵃᵇ	CD
4QpNah	Demetrius, Antiochus, the lion, the furious young lion, Seekers-After-Smooth things, Ephraim, Manasseh, Judah, House of Peleg, Kittim	4QpIsaᵃ, 4QpHosᵇ, 1QpHab, 4QpPsᵃ, 1QpPs	CD, 1QHᵃ, 1QM. 4Q285, 4Q177
1QpHab	Teacher of Righteousness, Liar, Kittim, House of Absalom, Wicked Priest, last priests of	4QpIsaᵃ ᵈ ᵉ, 1QpMic, 4QpNah, 4QpHosᵃ,	CD, 1QHᵃ, 1QM. 4Q285

Pesher	Personalities, events, sobriquets	Other pesharim	Other Qumran texts
	Jerusalem (see Table 2.2 for full content)		
1QpZeph	Mutilated commentary		
4QpZeph	Mutilated commentary		
1QpPs	Kittim?	4QpIsa[a], 4QpNah, 1QpHab	CD, 1QH[a], 1QM. 4Q285
4QpPs[a]	Teacher of Righteousness, Wicked Priest, Liar, congregation of the poor, ruthless ones of the covenant, house of Judah, Ephraim, Manasseh, council of the community	4QpIsa[d,e], 1QpMic, 4QpNah, 1QpHab, 4QpPs[b]	CD, 1QH[a]
4QpPs[b]	Teacher of Righteousness	1QpMic, 1QpHab, 4QpPs[a]	CD

As previously noted (Lim 1997a: 132-34 and 2000b: 63-65), four (4QpIsa[a,b,c,e]) of the five Isaiah pesharim have a higher ratio of biblical quotation to comment. Here, it may be added that 1QpZeph appears to follow this tendency. The citation of other biblical passages in 4QpIsa[c] has no counterpart in any other pesher. It has been suggested recently that this third pesher to Isaiah falls between the categories of the thematic and continuous pesharim (Lim 1991: 105 and independently by Bernstein 1994: 69-70). 4QpIsa[d], followed by 4QpIsa[a], conforms most closely, both in exegetical method and thematic content, to the model of pesher exegesis often discussed by scholarship and as represented in some of the passages from 1QpHab and 4QpPs[a]. The eschatological battle envisioned in 4QpIsa[a], headed by the Prince of the Congregation, has numerous thematic links in other Qumran scrolls, but none among the pesharim.

Not unexpectedly, 1QpHab shares exegetical and thematic features with almost all the pesharim. Significantly, it does not mention 'the lion of wrath' (Alexander Janneus) and 'Ephraim' (Pharisees) who figure prominently in the group of 4QpHos[b], 4QpNah and 4QpPs[a]. There is a range of exegeses framed within the Habakkuk Pesher. Alongside the well-known contemporizing turns are rather mundane paraphrases of the woes on idolatry at the end of Hab. 2.18-20. This is also evident in 4QpPs[a] where the commentary varies from the identification of biblical figures to a rewording of Ps. 37.39 (Lim 2000b: 63-64). The conflict between the Teacher of Righteousness, the Wicked Priest and the Liar is documented only in 1QpHab and 4QpPs[a], but the mention of the community's chosen priest occurs in two other pesharim, 1QpMic and 4QpPs[b]. The Kittim feature prominently in the Habakkuk pesher and 4QpIsa[a], but not in 4QpNah and 1QpPs. 1QpHab's use of scribal marks is, so far as one knows, not reflected in any other pesher. But the practice of leaving spacers between lemma and comment is not unique to these scribes as evidenced by similar codicological features in 4QpIsa[a], 4QpHos[a], 4QpNah and 4QpPs[a]. Together with 1QpMic and 1QpZeph, 1QpHab writes the four letters of the name of God in palaeo-Hebrew script, a practice that is also evidenced in some of the biblical scrolls.

The historical references in 4QpNah to Demetrius and Antiochus are unparalleled in the pesharim, so is the name 'Seekers-After-Smooth-Things' as a sobriquet for the Pharisees (though found in 4Q177). The House of Peleg is mentioned only here among the pesharim (cf. CD 20.22). The mixing of historical and coded references appears to be inspired by the biblical text where the oracles of Nahum name Assyria and Nineveh but also refer to them symbolically as 'lions' and 'young lions'. 4QpNah has a greater proportion of segmentation than any other pesher. Notable, it shares with the Habakkuk Pesher a polysemic approach to the biblical text (cf. 'lion' in 4QpNah and 'traitors/nations' in 1QpHab col. 2).

Pesher as a literary genre is more diverse than has been previously recognized. Built upon the common elements of lemma, interpretative formula and comment, each pesher is similar to and different from other pesharim in the use of various exegetical methods and the focus upon certain topics and figures. Deconstructing this scholarly genre would be going too far, but the recognition of its diversity is the first step towards a better understanding of the literary form.

3

THE GENRE OF PESHER: DEFINITION AND CATEGORIZATION

From the earliest publications of the Habakkuk Pesher to the present, scholars have correctly felt the need to relate this new genre of exegesis to those previously known. There have been comparisons with the Aramaic targumim (Brownlee 1955; Wieder 1953; Geza Vermes 1989: 188), the Demotic Chronicle (Rabin 1955: 148ff.), New Testament exegesis (Stendahl 1954; Ellis 1957) and rabbinic midrashim (e.g. Seeligmann 1953; Bruce 1959; Slomovic 1969). Of these, the comparative studies with the rabbinic midrashim have been prominent. For example, W.H. Brownlee (1951), the principal editor, proposed 13 hermeneutical principles or presuppositions of 1QpHab:

1. Everything the ancient prophet wrote has a *veiled, eschatological meaning*.
2. Since the ancient prophet wrote cryptically, his meaning is often to be ascertained through a *forced, or abnormal construction of the biblical text*.
3. The prophet's meaning may be detected through the study of the *textual or orthographic peculiarities* in the transmitted text. Thus the interpretation frequently turns upon the special readings of the text cited.
4. A *textual variant*, that is, a different reading from the one cited, may also assist interpretation.
5. The application of the features of a verse may be determined by *analogous circumstances*, or by
6. *Allegorical propriety*.
7. For the full meaning of the prophet, *more than one meaning may be attached to his words*.
8. In some case the original prophet so completely veiled his meaning that he can be understood only by an *equation of synonyms*, attaching to the original word a secondary meaning of one of its synonyms.

9. Sometimes the prophet veiled his message by writing one word instead of another, the interpreter being able to record the prophet's meaning by a *rearrangement of the letters in a word*, or by

10. The *substitution of similar letters* for one or more of the letters in the word of the biblical text.

11. Sometimes the prophet's meaning is to be derived by *the division of one word into two or more parts, and by expounding the parts*.

12. At times the original prophet concealed his message beneath abbreviations, so that the cryptic meaning of a word is to be evolved through *interpretation of words, or parts of words, as abbreviations*.

13. Other *passages of Scripture* may illumine the meaning of the original prophet.

Several scholars have criticized Brownlee's schematization of the pesherite hermeneutics (e.g. Elliger1953: 157-64; Horgan 1979: 250 n. 84; and Nitzan 1986: 34-39). George J. Brooke (1985: 283-92), for instance, has pointed out that Brownlee failed to distinguish between hermeneutics (no. 1)—the principles and presuppositions of the ancient interpreter—from the exegetical techniques and devices used to interpret the biblical texts (nos. 2-13). It was also felt by many that Brownlee's principles, especially the total of 13 in all, were artificial (see, e.g., separation of nos. 5 and 6 into two different categories) and tendentious, suspiciously similar to the *middot* of Rabbi Ishmael which are themselves abstractions of what the *darshan* was actually doing (see Alexander 1983 and 1984 for discussions of the *middot*).

Karl Elliger, moreover, argued that although the interpretations are fixed to particular texts and that the pesherite method has similarities to midrashic techniques, the meaning is essentially derived from revelation: 'Its interpretation grounds itself not on the text alone, but in greater measure and at decisive points upon a particular revelation' (1953: 155). Elliger stressed the terminological and exegetical similarity of the Habakkuk pesher to the interpretation of dreams and visions in Daniel (see also Finkel 1963–64). Oppenheim (1956) has extended the comparison to other dream interpretations in the ancient Near East.

Based on the works of Brownlee and Elliger, numerous studies have tried to extend and reconcile the two perspectives. Notwithstanding the 13 hermeneutical principles, many have sought to correct and amplify the pesherite techniques by comparison with midrashic ones (e.g. Rabinowitz 1973; Nitzan 1986: 29-79). Several rabbinic techniques have been discussed (e.g. *gezerah shevah* 'argument from analogy'), although some of them are more imagined than real (e.g. *'al tiqrê...'elā*, 'do not read x...but y'; cf. Lim 1997a: 128).

Silberman (1961) attempted to reconcile Brownlee's midrashic hermeneutical principles with Elliger's revelatory approach. He argued that while the Habakkuk pesher 'itself offers a theory of revelatory interpretation, in practice its interpretations are in large measure identical with literary devices used in many of the early midrashim where no such claim is made'. This has been followed by Miller (1971: 53) and Brooke (1985: 5). Silberman suggested that in both structure and presuppositions the Habakkuk pesher can be compared to the petirah midrashim (see now Niehoff 1992).

1. The Thematic Pesharim

In his 1970 study on 11QMelchizedek, Jean Carmignac refined the genre when he distinguished between two types of pesharim, the *'pesher continu'* and the *'pesher discontinu'* or *'thématique'*. The former category is 'the continuous pesher' which was discussed in the previous chapter. The latter, a type of pesher which he characterized as a text where 'the author chooses for himself the biblical texts which lend themselves to his intepretation' (Carmignac 1969–71: 361).

By contrast to the continuous pesher that systematically follows, 'bit by bit', the order of the biblical text, the thematic pesher is organized around a central idea. Thus, for 11QMelchizedek, Carmignac argued that the author of this thematic pesher drew on diverse biblical texts (Deut .15.2, Ps. 82.2, Isa. 52.7) to support the central idea, not about Melchizedek *per se*, but 'the deliverance of the just'. To be sure the heavenly redeemer figure of Melchizedek will play a certain role, but it is the deliverance from the dominion of Belial that is the central theme. Carmignac pointed to 4Q174, 4Q177 and 4Q182 and others as examples of this genre and conferred the name of 'thematic pesharim' upon them in preference over their designations as 'florilegium' (or anthology) and 'catena' ('chain of quotations').

The identification of the theme of 11QMelchizedek is straightforward, even if one quibbles over whether the thematic centre should lie in the role of Melchizedek himself or the salvific process. What is not so simple to articulate are the themes of 4QFlor, 4QCatena[a] and 4QCatena[b]. Does 4QFlor revolve around the theme of the eschatological Temple or the notion of the last days? It is evident that the phrase 'in the last days' (*be'aḥarit ha-yamim*) recurs throughout 4QCatena[a] (as noted by Strugnell 1969–71: 236-37 and developed by Steudel 1994: 163-69), but if this is a theme, then it is odd that it should become definitive for this putative genre of 'Midrash Eschatology'. After all, as Steudel herself pointed out, the phrase *be'aḥarit ha-yamim*, which she translated as 'the final period of history', occurs 33 times in the scrolls, not only in 4Q174 and 4Q177, but also in the continuous pesharim (1QpHab, 4QpIsa[a-d], 4QpNah) and other scrolls (4Q178, 4Q182, 4Q252, 4QDibHam[a], 4QMMT, CD and 11QMelch; Steudel 1993: 227 n. 12).

Recently, I have suggested that 4Q177 along with 4Q158, 4Q175 (4QTestimonia) and 4Q176 (4QTanh) were biblical anthologies with comments that may have originally been used for private devotion or disputation. This was based upon Edwin Hatch's conception of biblical *excerpta* in his Grinfield lecture (1889: 203). Although it has sometimes been wrongly seen to be the origin of 'the testimony book' hypothesis (e.g. Harnack 1958: 175 n. 1), Hatch's view (which he developed only in relation to Romans 3) is in fact quite distinctive in positing collections, and not simply one book, among Jews and not Christians (1997: 149-58). Annette Steudel sensed this connection too when she noted the affinities between 4Q177 and 4QTest: 'There are hints in 4Q177 that testimonies, collections of quotations, were used' (1990: 480, n. 24). But she rejected Allegro's designation because it did not fit the examples of catena in the Middle Ages and instead opted for the genre of 'Eschatological Midrash'.

Biblical *excerpta*, as hypothesized by Hatch, is a better formulation than the theologically loaded term of 'testimony' that presupposes Christian apologetics (the terminology is derived from Cyprian's *ad Quirinum: Testimoniorum libri tres*). The biblical excerpts that Hatch found were embedded in the writings of the apostolic fathers, and not in the mediaeval period, and were thought to belong originally to manuals of controversy and devotion. These lists of biblical passages were diverse in content: on peace based upon piety (*1 Clem.* 15); on good works (*1 Clem.* 34.6); on love (*1 Clem.* 50); humility (*1 Clem.* 56); Christ's fulfilment of Scripture (*1 Clem.* 22); Christ's passion (*Barn.* 5.13); baptismal liturgy (*Barn.* 11); and Temple theology (*Barn.* 16.2). Manuals of controversy are evidenced in the biblical extracts embedded in Justin's *Dialogue with Trypho* and his *First Apology*.

I have suggested that earlier examples may be found in the chains of scriptural quotations embedded in the letters of Paul (Rom. 3.10-18; 9.25-29; 11.33-36; 15.9-12, 11-13, 15-21; 11.8-10; 12.19-20; Gal. 4.27-30; 1 Cor. 3.19-20 and 2 Cor. 9.9-10) and that on one occasion the *excerpta* overlapped: 2 Sam. 7.14 is cited in both 4Q174 and 2 Cor. 6.14–7.1 (which some scholars believe is an 'Essene interpolation'). Based upon 4QTest, I argued that one of the features of this postulate of biblical *excerpta* is diversity of format and theme. They were written on single or multiple sheets, rather than on a codex or book, but in any case they must have been short enough to serve as handy collections. The theme may well be self-evident or opaque when viewed by a third party, as is the nature of notes, from ancient times to this day (Lim 1997a: 156-58).

Carmignac's identification of the thematic pesharim was endorsed and extended by Devorah Dimant who added a third and even fourth type of pesher (see also, Brooke 1990: 532). The 'isolated pesharim' are single quotations of one or more biblical verses which have been interpreted by the '*pesher* methods and terminology' in a text of a different literary genre (Dimant 1984: 504; 1992: 248). Dimant pointed to examples of this type in what she called a *pesher* on Zech. 13.7 in CD 19.5-13, a *pesher* on Amos 5.26-27 in CD 7.14-19, a *pesher* on Isa. 40.3 in 1QS 8.13-15, and other passages in CD. But the technical term *pesher* only occurs in the commentary on Isa. 24.17 in CD 4.15 and not in the passages mentioned by Dimant. Assumed in Dimant's third category, therefore, is a definition of the genre that does not require the use of the term 'pesher'. She takes as understood a definition of pesher.

Dimant also considered the use of sobriquets and allusions as other forms of pesher. For example, the disparaging nickname that the Qumran community gave to the Pharisees is 'the Seekers-After-Smooth-Things' and this is based upon an implied interpretation of Isa. 30.8-14 (Dimant 1992: 248). A very similar line of reasoning is also suggested in Bilhah Nitzan's commentary (1986: 43-46) and in Menahem Kister's (1992) study of hidden biblical interpretations. It is surely correct to observe that epithets and other biblical allusions play an important role in the matrix of the continuous pesher and that these may have been based upon exegesis of whole passages, but to call these phenomena 'pesharim', 'pesher-like' when neither the technical term nor even the exegesis is present is surely going too far. Why does 'pesher' exegesis have such privilege?

2. Midrash

As mentioned above, comparisons between the pesherite and midrashic techniques have been drawn since the early days of Qumran research. Most scholars stop short of calling 1QpHab a 'midrash'. In William H. Brownlee's 1979 commentary, however, he suggested that the genre of 1QpHab is 'midrash pesher' (1979: 23-28; already anticipated earlier in Brownlee 1951: 54-76). The sole evidence of this putative genre, a hybrid literary form of 'pesher' and 'midrash', is to be found in the occurrence of both terms in frag. 1, line 14 'Explanation of (*midrash*) How *blessed is the man who does not walk in the counsel of the wicked* (Ps. 1.1). Interpreted (*pesher*), this saying [concerns] those who turn aside from the way [of the people]' (restoration after Knibb, 1987: 259 and 261).

It is an odd use of midrash (Lim 1997b; Alexander 2000: 43 n. 15) and the two terms seem to be redundant. For Brownlee, however, 'midrash' is understood in its titular sense and belongs to the *incipit* that describes this entire section. Extrapolating this to 1QpHab, he concluded that '1QpHab is indeed a midrash; and if one wishes to characterize it further, he may qualify it appropriately as midrash pesher' (1979: 25).

In the Qumran scrolls, the term 'midrash' has several connotations:

communal study (1QS 8.14-16; 8.26); judicial inquiry (1QS 6.24); communal regulation (CD 20.6; 4QD[a] [4Q266], frag 18, col. 5.18-20); and a title for the authoritative interpretation (4QS[d] [4Q258]; frag 1, col. 1.1 'midrash for the Maskil'; 4QS[b] [4Q256], frag 5, col. 1.1; compare 1QS 5.1 where the variant title reads 'this is the rule for the men of the community'; see Lim 1997b: 285-90).

The titular use of the term also occurs on the title page, written on the verso, or back, of a recently published text known as 'Midrash Sepher Moshe'. Stephen Pfann (1999), the editor of the 4Q249, suggested that this composition is related to the 'midrash ha-Torah' of 1QS 8.15 and that the latter may have referred to actual written compositions proceeding from the Community's nightly deliberations on 'the way' of the Torah (DJD, 35: 1-3). Unfortunately, the body of the text, written in cryptic script, is badly mutilated and one has very little idea of what this 'midrash' originally looked like.

The double occurrence of 'midrash' and 'pesher' in 4Q174 is puzzling. The phrase *midraš mîn* surely has to be translated as 'an explanation of'. One would expect this to be followed immediately by the comment that singles out 'the blessed man' of the biblical text with those who turn aside from the way of the people. Instead, there is a typical interpretative formula: *pēšer hadāvār*, 'the interpretation of the matter'. Such formulas with *pešer* usually introduce sectarian comments of a biblical text.

Is the phrase 'an explanation of' the beginning of a title as Brownlee suggested? The vacat or space at the end of the previous line does indeed suggest that line 14 is the beginning of a new section. But if this phrase, together with the quotation of Ps. 1.1, constitutes a title, then it would be very awkward indeed for the body of this midrash to begin with *pēšer hadāvār*, 'the interpretation of the matter (or verse)', a stereotyped formula that occurs in the continuous pesharim to introduce a sectarian comment on a biblical verse. It is unlikely that something has dropped out, since the sectarian comment is keyed to the biblical text of Ps. 1.1.

Michael Knibb has drawn attention to the similarity of language between 4QFlor and that found in CD 8.16 = 19.29 and 1QSa 1.2b-3a in his reconstruction of line 14: 'those who turn aside from the way [of the people]' (1987: 261 and 69). Both in CD and 1QSa the reference is to the converts of Israel, the former to the members of the movement and the latter to the eschatological congregation. Though Knibb does not draw this conclusion, there may have been a tradition of communal regulation being referred to. CD 8.16 (=19.26) interprets a combined quotation of Deut. 9.5a and 7.8a with an introductory formula, 'thus is the judgment' (*kēn ha-mišpaṭ*), and 1QSa 1.2b-3 is part of 'the rule' (*ha-serekh*) for the whole congregation.

If this is correct, then the pesher of 4QFlor is commenting on a pre-existent tradition that already interpreted passages in Deuteronomy and

Psalms to be references to the converts of Israel. Perhaps this tradition originated from the study of the community and has since become part of the communal regulation. 'Midrash', in this view, would refer to the content of the community's study, and 'pesher' would be an interpretation of not just Ps. 1.1 but also its accompanying tradition. The collocation of other biblical texts (Isa. 8.11 and Ezek. 44.10) with pithy comments is indicative of this external reference: 'they are those about whom it is written in the book of Ezekiel the prophet' and 'they are the sons of Zadok and the m[e] of [their] council'.

If this is right, then the evidence for a genre of 'midrash pesher' vanishes, since the 'pesher' in 4QFlor is an interpretation of a pre-existent sectarian explanation of Ps. 1.1 based perhaps upon their nightly deliberations. It is no evidence for the existence of a genre of 'midrash pesher'.

One of the most methodologically conscious studies on the genre of the Qumran pesher was undertaken by George J. Brooke (1979–80). Beginning with a short history of scholarship and discussion of form-critical considerations, Brooke correctly underscored the importance of exegetical structure over techniques of interpretation, arguing that the devices identified by scholars as midrashic are secondary and 'not constitutive of the genre pesher' (p. 496). Instead, he focused on the primary factor of 'structural combination': (1) biblical quotation; and (2) interpretation that includes identification and explanation. On this basis, Brooke argued that the same structure can be discerned across the biblical interpretation of three different texts: Amos 5.27 in CD 7.14b-21a; 2 Samuel 7 in 4QFlor col. 1, lines 10-13; Hab. 1.17 in 1QpHab 6.8-12; and Hab. 2.17 in 1QpHab 12.1-10. He concluded that the Qumran commentaries ought 'to be properly classified as *Qumran midrash*' (p. 502) and pesher as a 'sub-genre', adding that 'it may well be preferable to drop the word and all its associated complications that are too often forgotten' (p. 503). For Brooke, the presence of the term *pesher* is not a requirement for the identification of the genre and the word 'is not structurally necessary since personal or demonstrative pronouns can serve the same purpose' (p. 487). Most recently, Brooke (2000c: 298), seems to have moved away from the notion of the *Qumran midrash*, stating that '[t]he use of the term *midrash* in iii.14 [i.e. of 4QFlor] seems to be technical, not referring to a literary genre (as the later rabbinic *midrashim*), but identifying a method of scriptural exposition'.

Brooke's emphasis upon structure has been corroborated by the discussion in Chapter 1 on the common elements of the continuous pesharim. The move away from the literary genre of 'Qumran midrash' is also welcome. To be sure, exegetical techniques and devices between the Qumran pesharim can also be found in other scrolls (see Lim 2000b: 64) and rabbinic midrashim, but to call the pesher not as 'pesher' but as 'Qumran midrash' is to privilege a term used only once in the exegetical scrolls over another that is prevalent.

3. Midrash Eschatology

Annette Steudel, more than anyone else, has been responsible for the introduction of a genre called 'Midrash Eschatology' into scholarship. Following in the footsteps of her *Doktorvater*, Hartmut Stegemann, who defined 4QPatriachal Blessings or 4Q252 as the literary genre of 'thematic Midrash' (1967: 193-227), Steudel proposed that 4Q174 together with 4Q177 can be classified as a 'Midrash Eschatology' (1994: 190-92). She also suggested that the 4Q182, 4Q178 and 4Q183 possibly belong to the same genre, but correctly refrained from drawing definite conclusions from these badly preserved fragments (Steudel 1994: 152-57). As already noted above, the reconstruction of 4Q174 and 4Q177 as two copies, by different scribes, of the same scroll is possible but not compelling since there is no textual overlap. The obvious alternative is that they are two copies of two different texts that are similar to each other.

According to Steudel, 'Midrash Eschatology' is moreover a 'thematic midrash' which is equivalent to Carmignac's '*pesher thématique*'. But 'midrash' occurs only once in the phrase 'explanation of' in 4Q174 and it is to be doubted that it is the heading of an embedded genre of 'midrash'. It is perhaps a reference to a pre-existent tradition about the converts of Israel.

In the history of scholarship, the contemporary designation of ancient exegesis as 'midrash' can be traced to Geza Vermes (1961) (so Alexander 2000: 35) who drew on the pioneering efforts of Renée Bloch. Scholars were and continue to be divided about calling pre-rabbinic exegesis 'midrashic'. Differences arose regarding the degree of adherence to the terminology and forms of rabbinic midrashim: those who preferred a strict definition would insist on evidence for the use of the term in its technical rabbinic sense; some see the similarities of hermeneutics and exegetical techniques between the pesher and rabbinic midrashim as evidence of the continuity and persistence of Jewish biblical interpretation; yet others have argued that 'midrash', as used in scholarship, has become such an elastic term that it has been emptied of any meaning—it has become no more than a sexy synonym for interpretation!

Recently, Philip Alexander has pointed out that the term 'midrash' is fundamentally ambiguous 'even within its narrower rabbinic usage, since it denotes both a hermeneutical method and a concrete text which exemplifies that method and is cast in the literary form of lemma plus comment' (2000: 37). He noted that 'Midrash' is now commonly applied to the whole of Second Temple biblical interpretation and this midrashic period is to be distinguished from the next phase of Jewish Bible commentary known as *parshanut*. Midrash in this looser sense characterizes a text no more precisely than calling it 'an example of early Jewish Bible interpretation' (Alexander 2000: 37 n. 5). However, he cautioned against an unreflected homogenization of the rabbinic and Qumran styles of exegesis in the invocation of the word 'midrash'.

When Steudel described her reconstruction of 4Q174 and 4Q177 as 'A Midrash on Eschatology' she had a specific meaning. It is clearly not 'midrash' in the generic sense of the term. This hard sense of the word is questionable and, to paraphrase Alexander, blurs the distinctions between the Qumran and rabbinic types of exegesis.

4. Pesher as a Distinct Genre

Pesher is best seen as a distinct genre of exegesis; as such it is neither generic nor unique. It uses exegetical techniques and devices that are also found in the rabbinic midrashim and in much of Second Temple biblical interpretation and beyond. It is better to regard pesher to be falling on the exegetical continuum that begins within the scriptural tradition itself, a phenomenon well described by Michael Fishbane (1988) as inner biblical interpretation, and continues to the rabbinic midrashim and beyond. Within this continuum other ancient exegeses should also be set, like the Targumim and Pauline and other New Testament interpretation of Scripture.

The common pesherite structure identified in the last chapter, namely the lemma, introductory formula with or without the technical term and comment, is paralleled in the rabbinic midrashim, but also elsewhere. Yet, the pesher is not a generic form of biblical exegesis. The content of the pesher, even if it is not constitutive of the genre, marks it out from other exegesis, both in its emphasis upon prophetic literature (including the Psalms), eschatological orientation, contemporizing tendencies and the special role that it confers upon a continuous revelation and the Teacher of Righteousness.

As a genre, the pesher reflects a common exegetical approach to the scriptural text: the consecutive citation of verses from a section of biblical passages is interspersed with comments, much like the way some modern commentaries present their verse-by-verse exposition by first quoting and then commenting on each biblical verse. Also, like its modern counterparts, the pesher can isolate specific phrases or words from the biblical text for comment by re-citation in the body of the comment. Thus, in the example of 1QpHab 6-7, the pesherist highlights his interpretative concerns by quoting again the phrase '*that he who reads it may read it speedily*' (Hab. 2.2) in the body of the comment. But built upon this common exegetical approach is a range of techniques and devices.

Pesher as a genre of scriptural interpretation is a scholarly construct. There is no ancient list of the 15 texts enumerated in Chapter 1 as a collection of 'pesharim'. In fact, the term *pesher* never occurs in titular form in a continuous pesher, in the way that 'midrash' has now been found as a title. It is an assumption, and one that is widely held, that the Qumranians would themselves have recognized these texts as pesharim.

'Pesher' can also refer to a method of exegesis rather than a genre of biblical interpretation. The technical term is used in texts that are manifestly not 'a pesher', as, say, in the interpretation of Isa. 24.17 in the Damascus Document (CD 4.14):

> During all those years Satan shall be unleashed against Israel, as He spoke by the hand of Isaiah, son of Amoz, saying, *Terror and the pit and the snare are upon you, O inhabitant of the land* (Isa. 24.17). Interpreted (*pišro*), these are the three nets of Satan with which Levi son of Jacob said that he catches Israel by setting them up as three kinds of righteousness. The first is fornication, the second is riches and the third is profanation of the Temple.

Here, the three elements of the biblical verse, 'terror', 'the pit' and 'the snare' are interpreted as 'the three nets of Satan (or Belial)' set up deceptively as three kinds of righteousness in order to ensnare Israel. Alternatively this 'isolated pesher' can be viewed as a citation of a passage from a continuous pesher to Isaiah.

As a method of exegesis, 'pesher' is also used to explicate a concept (e.g. 'ages of creation' in 4Q180), a biblical law (Lev. 16.1 in 4Q159, frag. 5) and possibly the promise to Abraham (4Q464).

If the sub-genre of 'thematic pesher' describes any text at all, it would be 11QMelch, since there is a prominent theme in the text. The other scrolls considered under this secondary category do not exhibit the same thematic clarity and may have been loose collections of biblical excerpts with short comments.

4

BIBLICAL QUOTATIONS IN THE PESHARIM

The nature of the biblical quotations embedded in the continuous pesharim preoccupied scholars in the early days of Qumran research. Excitement centred on the way the then newly published 1QpHab enriched its commentary on the biblical text of Habakkuk by reference to readings in textual traditions other than the MT. An example, which became a *locus classicus* or paradigmatic passage for illustrating this phenomenon (see, e.g., already in G. Vermes' dictionary article, 'Interpretation, History', 441), is seen in the citation of and comment on Hab. 2.16 in col. 11, ll. 8-15:

> *You have filled yourself with ignominy more than with glory. Drink also, and stagger! The cup of the Lord's right hand shall come round to you and shame shall come on your glory* (Hab. 2.16). Interpreted, this concerns the Priest whose ignominy was greater than his glory. For he did not circumcise the foreskin of his heart, and he walked in the ways of drunkeness that he might quench his thirst. But the cup of the wrath of God shall confuse him, multiplying his… and the pain of…

What struck the first generation of Qumran scholars was the different reading of the second sentence which can be literally translated as:

> 1QpHab   *Drink also you and stagger (hērā'ēl)*
> MT   *Drink also you and be uncircumcised (hē'ārēl)*

Here was a 'variant' from the traditional Hebrew text which resolved the awkwardness of the MT. An emendation to this reading was already suggested by as eminent a figure as Julius Welhausen, followed by many, long before the Habakkuk pesher had been discovered among the first seven scrolls in 1947 (Welhausen 1898: 169). As a variant, the pesherite 'stagger' fit the context better than 'be uncircumcised' of the MT. It was evident that the pesherite *hērā'ēl* was not due to a scribal error of metathesis (i.e. the transposition of the letters *resh* and *ayin*), since the comment relies on the variant reading when it speaks about walking 'in the ways of drunkeness' and the quenching of the Priest's thirst. This variant is supported by the double translation of 'staggering and tottering' in the LXX. Moreover, it seemed that the Qumran commentator also knew the reading of the MT when he referred to the uncircumcision of the foreskin of his heart (*'orlat libô*). There was, as it were, an internal discourse between the readings of 'uncircumcision' and 'stagger' and between the lemma and the interpretation.

By 1959, the intense interest in the pesherite biblical quotation had reached its zenith, following the scholarly treatments by J. van der Ploeg (1951), Georg Molin (1952), Karl Elliger (1953), Stanislav Segert (1953–55), William Brownlee (1951, 1955 and especially 1959) and others. In that year, Brownlee declared that 'our [i.e. Elliger, Segert and his own] discussion of each variant in turn has made further discussion of most of the textual variants [in the Habakkuk Pesher] unnecessary' (1959: 96).

From 1960 onwards, it seemed that scholarly attention did on the whole turn away from the nature of the biblical quotations of the Habakkuk Pesher to its exegesis. To be sure there continued to be publications on the biblical quotations, but these were either exceptional (e.g., Vegas Montaner 1989), were concerned with other pesharim (e.g. Weiss 1963–64; Vegas Montaner 1980; Sinclair 1983; Brooke 1987), or were of a more general nature (e.g. Gabrion 1979). This turning point coincided with the introduction, in roughly the same period, of midrash as a term to describe pre-rabbinic Jewish exegeses (see Chapter 3).

One of the reasons for this shift can be traced to the widely held belief that the pesherist biblical quotations included exegetical variants. The biblical quotations were not seen to represent any textual tradition. A frequently discussed variant occurs at the beginning of col. 11 of 1QpHab. In the passage immediately preceeding the above gobbet, a sectarian reading appears to have been used:

> Woe to him who causes his neighbours to drink; who pours out his venom to make them drunk that he may gaze on their feast! (Hab. 2.15). Interpreted, this concerns the Wicked Priest who pursued the Teacher of Righteousness to the house of his exile that he might confuse him with his venomous fury. And at the time appointed for rest, for the Day of Atonement, he appeared before them to confuse them, and to cause them to stumble on the Day of Fasting, their Sabbath of repose (1QpHab 11.2-8).

The final phrase of Hab. 2.15 literally reads as follows:

> 1QpHab   *in order to look upon their feasts* (mo'adeyhem)
> MT   *in order to look upon their nakedness* (me'oryhem)

In Hebrew, the difference between the two words is not to be found only in the interchange of the position of the letter *ayin*, but in the reading of a *dalet* for a *resh*. The pesherite variant is not a scribal mistake, because the commentary assumes this reading. The Wicked Priest pursued the Teacher of Righteousness to his house of exile on the day of Atonement and he is able to do so and not be required to perform cultic rites at the Temple, because it was not *his* Yom Kippurim. As pointed out long ago by Shemaryahu Talmon, this passage indirectly evidences the implicit dispute between the Qumran community and the Temple of Jerusalem over the calendar (1951: 549-63). The phrase, 'and at the time appointed', is translated literally as 'at the end of the feast (*mo'ed*)' (line 3).

In Karl Elliger's edition of the Hebrew text of the minor prophets, 'their feasts' for Hab. 2.15 was considered a possible textual variant (see *BHS*: 1052, critical apparatus). Many scholars, however, thought otherwise and took it not just as an exegetical variant, but a sectarian one. In 1QH 12.11-12 (formerly col. 4) the opponents of the speaker (the one referred to as 'I' in these thanksgiving hymns), now frequently identified with the Teacher of Righteousness, are described as those who 'gaze on their straying, on their folly concerning feast-days (*bemo'adeyhem*), on their fall into their snares'. Since this reading is unattested outside the Qumran scrolls, so far as one is aware, it was thought that it must have been a variant that reflected the sectarian concerns of feasts and calendars rather than a textual variant.

Another much discussed exegetical modification is the reading of 'riches' for 'wine' in Hab. 2.5 of 1QpHab 8.3. The Hebrew of the relevant phrase differs from the MT in several respects and can be translated with Vermes as '*Moreover, the arrogant man seizes wealth*', the subject of the imperfect verb (*yivgōd*) being *gever yāhîr*. The MT has the participle *boged* and the noun *ha-yyayin* ('wine'). In 1QpHab, however, the reading is either *hwn* or *hyn*, the *waw* and *yod* are indistinguishable. After initial discussions about the various ways of understanding this cluster of unpointed consonants—including its possible vocalization as *Hayyan*, an Ugaritic name (W. F. Albright cited in Brownlee 1959: 48-49)—most scholars read *hôn*, since 'wealth' (with the article) is considered by CD as the second of three 'nets of Belial' (4.17). Moreover, it was suggested that the original reading was *ha-yyayin* and that the pesherist had changed this to *hôn* by the technique of *'al tiqrê...'elā* ('do not read X, but Y') in order to suit the sectarian concern that wealth was one of the three nets of Belial (e.g., among many others, Finkel 1963–64: 257; and Slomovic 1969: 3-15).

There are several difficulties with this view:

1. The reading *ha-hon* as 'wealth' is problematic in CD 4-5, since it (unlike the first and third 'nets') is not interpreted. The late Jonas Greenfield (with Emile Puech) had argued that the reading should be *ha-hyn* and this was a misreading of *pahaz* or *pahuz* if one thinks

in terms of the Qumran bookhand (Greenfield 1988). This view is not widely accepted, though to its credit it does attempt to resolve, rather than gloss over, the difficulties of CD 4-5.

2.   The expansive translation of the Peshitta, 'a presumptious and avaricious man does not become satisfied', corroborates the pesherite reading, as pointed out long ago by Krister Stendahl (1954: 188). If 'wealth' is a sectarian reading, then it is so only in the limited sense that both 1QpHab and CD drew upon a textual variant because it suited their concerns. The external evidence of the Peshitta militates against the view that the original reading was created by the pesherist from 'wine' to 'wealth'.

3.   The technique 'do not read X...but Y' requires by definition the presence of the Hebrew words *'al tiqrê...'elā*, but these are nowhere to be found. The further suggestion that there are implicit *'al tiqrê* exegeses that do not require these terms sets the entire issue beyond scholarly discourse and into the realm of the irrefutable.

1. On Identifying Exegetical Variants

The past few years have seen a renewed interest in the pesherite biblical quotations (see, e.g., H. Lichtenberger of the Institut für antikes Judentum und hellenistische Religionsgeschichte, Tübingen, and the project *Biblia Qumranica* that includes a comprehensive textual evaluation of the pesherite biblical quotations). In a study published in 1997, I raised questions about the way previous scholarship deemed a variant to be exegetical (Lim 1997a: 12-28). I approached the subject from two standpoints. First, the emerging consensus in post-Qumran textual criticism which posits a greater diversity of text-types than the tri- or bi-partite division of the Hebrew Bible has important ramifications for the way scholars identify a variant to be exegetical. Whether it be the multiple-text theory of Emanuel Tov (1992: 114-17) or the standard literary editions theory of Eugene Ulrich (2000: 73-81), the consequence of this textual diversity for exegesis has not been adequately recognized. The pluriformity of text-types serves as one of the key features of this new interpretative framework.

Secondly, a review of scholarship, undertaken in 1991 (Lim 1991: 29-52), showed that through no fault of their own scholars working in the early days of Qumran research did not recognize, and in fact could not have done so, the full implications of post-Qumran textual criticism. This was partly due to the nature of scholarship that looks backwards whence it has come. Pre-Qumran textual criticism was modelled on the tri- or bi-partite division of the Hebrew Bible into the proto-Masoretic Text (or now sometimes called the proto-Rabbinic text), the Greek translation of the LXX, and for the

Pentateuch and other biblical texts (by analogy) the Samaritan Pentateuch. Readings that deviate from these standards were seen to be exegetical variants, an assumption that cannot be sustained by the new framework of textual criticism. A reading could have been modified from, say, a proto-MT base text or maybe not, but either way it must be shown on a case-by-case basis and not simply assumed.

The specialization of scholarly interests and the separation of the scrolls into biblical and non-biblical texts have also contributed to the neglect. Until recently, most popular or more scholarly anthologies of the Dead Sea Scrolls select only non-biblical texts (see Lim 1997a: 15 for a survey). The assumption seems to be that the biblical texts belong to the technical business of textual criticism and not of general interest. This has now been remedied in part by the publication of *The Dead Sea Scrolls Bible* (Abegg, Flint and Ulrich: 1999), although its title and conception are problematic (see my review in Lim: 2001b: 759-61).

Until recently there has been no sustained discussion of how one identifies a variant in the Pesharim to be exegetical or textual. Apart from the odd comment here and there (e.g. see recently van der Kooij 2000: 106 *et passim*), scholars have for the most part refrained from spelling out how they know that a variant is exegetical or textual.

In the past decade, discussions arising out of the publication of a variant found in 4Q252 or 4QCommentary on Genesis A, have brought some of the issues to the fore. 4Q252 is not a continuous pesher but it does use the technical term in one of its interpretative sections. It is a text of varied exegetical character that includes in the first two columns a chronology that dates important events of the flood story by the 364-day solar calendar known from Jubilees and other Qumran texts.

The contentious reading appears in the well-known opening lines of the commentary: '[In the] four hundred and eightieth year of Noah's life, their end came to Noah. And God said: 'My Spirit shall not dwell (*lō yādûr*) in man forever'' (Gen. 6.3). Is the reading 'shall not dwell' an exegetical or textual variant? The MT reads *lō yādôn*, a phrase which has been variously translated as will not 'strive', 'endure', 'humble', 'strong', 'govern', 'dwell' and most commonly 'judge'.

In my 1992 study of the chronology of the flood story, I noted in a passing comment that this is a variant attested by the LXX (Lim 1992b: 292). My suggestion was queried by Moshe Bernstein in an article published in the subsequent year (Bernstein 1993–94). Eight years later, I returned to this topic in an invited paper for the Scriptorium Conference at Hampton Court (Lim 2002a) in which I had the opportunity to examine this variant at length. I concluded that on balance, *yādûr* is probably a textual rather than an exegetical variant.

Although the full arguments should be consulted in the respective publications, the two approaches can be summarized in the following way. One considers *lō' yādûr* to be a contextual guess of *lō' yādôn*. Moshe Bernstein (1993–94) advocated the view that like Targum Onqelos, Jubilees, the Vulgate and the LXX, 4Q252 attempted to make sense of the problematic phrase. It does not attest to a textual variant in its paraphrase of Gen. 6.3. He assumed that the original reading was *lō yādôn* and the base text was the MT.

The second approach understands *lō yādûr* to be a textual variant because it belongs to a verbatim quotation (and not a paraphrase) in col. 1, line 2. External evidence, especially in the LXX and Philo, likely attests to the existence of a textual variant. I did not make any assumptions about the base-text of 4Q252 as a whole, a question which I considered to be a related, but distinct, issue.

Other scholars have expressed their views on the status of this reading. George J. Brooke (2000a: 112) and Ronald Hendel (2000: 838), for their own reasons, have concluded that *yādûr* is a textual variant.

Whatever one might think of *yādûr*, and the evidence and arguments are finely balanced, important methodological issues have been raised as a result. These include:

1. What was the original reading of 4Q252? Bernstein believes that it is *yādôn* as in the MT and *yādûr* is an exegetical guess. But how does he know that? The only reading found in col. 1 is *yādûr*. Is there any reason for needing to reconstruct a putative original? The alternative is to see it as the reading that the Qumran commentator had and *yādûr* as a textual variant of Gen. 6.3.

2. It is extremely difficult to distinguish between a close paraphrase from a verbatim quotation of a slightly variant text (Lim 1992b: 289). Is the phrase, 'my spirit will not dwell in man forever' a paraphrase or verbatim quotation? Bernstein argued that it is a paraphrase because there are no introductory formulas. But the phrase 'and God said' in lines 1-2 marks out the following as a direct quotation both in the MT and 4Q252. The question is where does the verbatim quotation end and paraphrase begin. I have suggested that the extent of the verbatim citation is 'My spirit shall not dwell in man forever' (so also Brooke, DJD, 22: 196).

3. How does one evaluate the evidence of the Septuagint or any other version? Bernstein argued that apart from Gen. 6.3 the Greek *katameinei* translates the Hebrew verbs *yāšab* (Num. 20.1; 22.9) or the verb *yā'al* in an expression (Josh 7.7), but never *dûr*. Conversely, the rare root *dwr* is translated in Ps. 84.11 by *oikeō* and not *katamenō*. The Septuagint translator, however, used the verb *oikeō*

not because it was the only possible translation of *dûr*, but that it allowed him to indulge in pun: the Psalmist would rather 'be cast aside in the house (*oikos*) of God rather than live (*oikein*) in tents of sinners' (Greek added to the translation by Pietersma 2000: 84). *katamenō* is a perfectly good verb to express the notion of 'dwelling' and Philo also independently attested to this use.

4.   George Brooke introduced a methodological principle into the discussion when he suggested that *yādûr* is likely to have been a textual variant because nothing exegetical depends on it (2000a: 111-12). By this, he means nothing lexically relies on it. While this rule of thumb generally holds true, it has its limits. Though *yādûr* may not have been exegetically used in the manner that, say, *mo'adêyhem* was lexically exploited in 1QpHab 11.2-8, it is semantically significant: 'my spirit will not judge (*yādôn*) in man forever' means that at some point God's present judgment will cease; whereas, 'my spirit will not dwell (*yādûr*) in man forever' announces an impending judgment by flood of waters in the form of the departure of the spirit of God. In 4Q252, it is the latter announcement of impending doom that inaugurates destruction by flood of waters.

Conversely, if exegesis depends upon a particular reading, does it necessarily mean that the variant is exegetical? This issue can be illustrated by another passage from 1QpHab 6.8-12:

> *Therefore their sword is ever drawn to massacre nations mercilessly* (Hab. 1.17). Interpreted, this concerns the Kittim who cause many to perish by the sword—youths, grown men, the aged, women and children—and who even take no pity on the fruit of the womb.

A passage that describes the ruthlessness of the Kittim or Romans, the biblical lemma contains an important variant. Literally, the first part of Hab 1.17 can be translated as follows:

> 1QpHab   *therefore he will empty his sword (ḥarbô) continually*
> MT   *therefore he will empty his net (ḥarmô) continually*

The exegesis of the passage depends upon the reading of 'sword' over 'net', as the Kittim are said to have caused many to perish 'by the sword' (*bāḥereb*, line 10). The two words are graphically similar. However, it is unlikely that this reading is exegetical, since it is also attested (*machairan autou*) in the Minor Prophet scroll from Nahal Hever (8HevXIIgr), dated to the time of the Habakkuk pesherist (c. 50 BCE).

Put differently, a reading that is exegetically significant, is not necessarily an exegetical variant. The ancient interpreter can, and does, incorporate pre-existent variants into his commentary. He could resort to exegetical modifications or simply draw upon the textual variants available to him.

Identifying variants as exegetical or textual in the biblical quotations has become more complicated in light of post-Qumran textual criticism. Each variant has to be assessed in its exegetical context and by evidence of external attestations. As I have previously suggested, the only sure way of knowing that a reading has been exegetically created is when the ancient commentator cites the same verse twice in two different ways (Lim 1997a: ch. 6). Such an example can be seen in the re-citation of Hab. 2.17 in 1QpHab 11.17–12.10:

> [*For the violence done to Lebanon shall overwhelm you, and the destruction of the beasts*] *shall terrify you, because of the blood of men and the violence done to the land, the city, and all its inhabitants* (Hab. 2.17). Interpreted, this saying concerns the Wicked Priest, inasmuch as he shall be paid the reward which he himself tendered to the Poor. For *Lebanon* is the Council of the Community; and the *beasts* are the Simple of Judah who keep the Law. As he himself plotted the destruction of the Poor, so will God condemn him to destruction. And as for that which He said, *Because of the blood of the city and the violence done to the land*: interpreted, *the city* is Jerusalem where the Wicked Priest committed abominable deeds and defiled the Temple of God. *The violence done to the land*: these are the cities of Judah where he robbed the Poor of their possessions.

Introduced by the formula, 'and as for that which He said', the second re-citation is an exegetically modified version of Hab. 2.17. The three citations literally read as follows:

First citation: *because of (the) blood of man and violence of land, town, and all who dwell in it* (12.1)

Second citation: *because of (the) blood of town and violence of land* (12.6-7)

Third citation: *and violence of land* (12.9)

The pesherist saw in the revealed words of Habakkuk references to the abomination of Jerusalem and her Temple and the cities of Judah which had been robbed by the Wicked Priest. He segmented the original lemma of Hab. 2.17, maintaining the wording of 'and violence of land' in the third citation. In the second citation, however, he altered the biblical text by changing 'blood of man' to 'blood of town', so that the modified form corresponded more closely with the defilement (by blood) of Jerusalem and the Temple. A literal or *peshat* reading of 'blood of man' will not allow him to make this connection easily.

One cannot be certain why the pesherist felt it necessary to alter his biblical text, rather than use some other technique or device, but perhaps part of the answer can be sought in the double occurrence of the text. The sentence, '*because of (the) blood of man and violence of land, town, and all who dwell in it*', occurs twice in the prophecy of Habakkuk, at 2.17 and earlier at 2.8. As

Hab. 2.18, the sentence was interpreted in col. 9.8-12 to be a reference to the Wicked Priest being handed over to his enemies on account of the 'wrong' done to the Teacher of Righteousness. The Hebrew of 'wrong' (*'avon*) usually means 'guilt', but in this context likely refers to some unspecified harm (perhaps involving bloodshed) done to the righteous Teacher.

For the Habakkuk pesherist, this sentence clearly has more than one sense.

It is a further example of how the ancient commentator regarded his biblical text to be imbued with more than one level of meaning. Because he had already interpreted the phrase 'because of (the) blood of man' in connection with the Wicked Priest's action against the Teacher of Righteousness in col. 9, it would appear that he decided to modify the text so that in col. 11 it now referred to the blood of the town of Jerusalem and its abomination of sacrifices at the Temple.

2. Textual Nature of Biblical Quotations Found in the Pesharim

Apart from Habakkuk in 1QpHab, the textual nature of the biblical quotations in the pesharim have not been thoroughly studied. There have been collations of variants (e.g. Vegas Montaner 1980) against the MT in the context of a methodological critique (e.g. Lim, 1997a: ch. 5), but these need to be supplemented by systematic textual comparisons with the LXX and other versions.

Such textual characterizations will have to take careful account of the exegetical characteristics of each pesher. As shown in Chapter 2, while sharing commonalities the continuous pesharim also exhibit diversity in exegetical techniques and approaches. The pesherist who wrote 1QpHab appears to have been much more intrusive in his approach to the Habakkuk text than, say, the exegete of 4QpIsa[b] (4Q162) whose comments are little more than glosses on large quotations of Isaiah. I have recently suggested that this second pesher to Isaiah is similar to the MT, with the one distinguishing feature that it is missing some nine verses of Isa. 5.15-24 (see Lim 2002a). This 'minus' cannot be explained by the incorrect joining of fragments (e.g. 4QpIsa[c]) or the selection of passages (e.g. 4QpPs[a] skips from Pss. 37 to 45 to 60). It appears to be missing from the text. But this suggestion needs to be complemented by a systematic textual comparison with all the relevant versions.

Habakkuk in 1QpHab is the only one that has been subjected to a thorough textual comparison and an eclectic theory of its text has been proposed. William Brownlee first advanced the view that prior to the composition of the Pesher, peculiar readings 'were discovered in some manuscript (or manuscripts) and were treated as authoritative' (1959: 115). As evidenced in the commentary, the ancient commentator was aware of variant readings for several verses and a reconstruction of his method could involve him reading various manuscripts side by side during composition. The eclectic nature of the Habakkuk text in 1QpHab has been corroborated by L. Vegas Montaner's more recent study of the variants in which he concluded that readings are scattered in one direction or another (1989: 318).

Krister Stendahl developed Brownlee's eclectic theory and stated that the Habakkuk text of 1QpHab 'certainly never existed as "a text" outside the commentary' and that the pesherist 'was conscious of various possibilities, tried them out, and allowed them to enrich its interpretation of the prophet's message' (1954: 194 and 190 respectively). Something similar may be proposed for 4QpNah and possibly also 4QpPs[a].

5

HISTORY IN THE PESHARIM

Though partially reconstructed, the references to '[Deme]trius' and 'Anti-ochus' in 4QpNah frags. 3-4, col. 1 give readers the clearest indication that the pesherist was indeed interested in history. His commentary was not just an exegetical and literary play on the words and oracles of the prophet Nahum, but in it was also a concern for contemporary life and events. The pesher genre has been described as exegesis 'from code to code', but this is only so if it is also kept in mind that on one occasion the regular use of cryptic language is abandoned in favour of naming historical figures.

Other Qumran scrolls corroborate the explicit references of the Nahum pesherist: 4Q322 frag. 2 preserves the names of 'Shelamzion' (Alexandra; wife of Alexander Jannaeus) and 'Hyrcanus' (II; their son); 4Q324a frag 2 4.8 includes the name 'Aemilius' (Scaurus; Pompey's general); 4Q324b frags. 1 and 2 refer to 'Shelamzion' and 'Johanan' (Hyrcanus II); and 4Q468g has a reference to 'Ptolais' or 'Ptolas', friend of Archelaus (so Broshi 1998: 345) or 'Peitholaus', the Jewish commander in Pompey's defeat of Aristobulus II (so W. Horbury, 1999; and D. Schwartz, 1999). It has also been argued that an ode to Alexander Jannaeus or Yannai can be read in the phrase, 'Holy City for King Jonathan and for all the congregation of Thy people' (4Q448, col. B, line 4; so, Eshel, Eshel and Yardeni 1992). But both the reading and its syntax have been queried by Philip Alexander (1993) and an alternative interpretation for Jonathan Maccabee has been advanced by G. Vermes (1993). In an independent study, A. Lemaire has tentatively concluded that this is a polemic *against*, and not a hymn for, Alexander Jannaeus (1997a: 70).

The cloak of secrecy was also dropped in a fragment concerning the rebuke of certain members of the Qumran community. Esther Eshel (1994) has suggested that 4Q477 is the guardian's register of rebukes of individuals who transgressed community rules. Much attention has been trained on the nature of one of the offences, whether it concerned 'the emission of the body' (Wise and Eisenman, 1992: 269-73) or sexual relations with a near kin

(Eshel 1994: following M. Broshi). Whatever the form of this sexual offence, it is notable that some of the members of the community, albeit miscreants, are named: 'Yohanan son of Ar...[they rebuked because] he was short-tempered'; 'They rebuked Hananiah Notos because he...[to dis]turb the spirit of the Community'; and '[they rebuked] Hananiah son of Sim[on] because he...'. This act of 'naming and shaming' of transgressors is in stark contrast to the familiar regulations, designating members as 'volunteers', 'the many', 'the community' and 'the congregation'.

The author of Pesher Nahum identified 'the lion' of Nah. 2.11b with a certain 'Demetrius' and, as discussed in Chapter 2, there is broad agreement that this individual was the Seleucid king Demetrius III Eucaerus (95–88 BCE) and the historical event in view was his aborted intervention into Judaean politics during the Jewish rebellion against Alexander Jannaeus (Josephus, *Ant.* 13.372-83 and *War* 1.90-8). The entire historical period was described by the pesherist in the phrase 'from the time of Antiochus until the coming of the rulers of the Kittim' (frags. 3-4, col. 1.3). The use of *myn* in the temporal sense of 'from the time of' is exceptional. Doubts have been raised concerning the identification of 'Antiochus' with Antiochus Epiphanes (175–164 BCE), since it was not during his rule, but that of Demetrius II (142 BCE), when Judaea gained political independence. In what sense did God keep Jerusalem from 'the power of the kings of Greece'? Maurya Horgan has plausibly suggested that the commentator may have been referring to religious, rather than political, freedom (1979: 174).

1. Sobriquets and Titles

All other historical references in Pesher Nahum and the remaining pesharim appear in the form of nicknames and titles. These sobriquets have already been discussed in Chapter 2, but certain ones need more extensive treatment.

1.1. The Kittim
4QpNah frags. 3-4, col. 1 describes how the kings of Greece (*malkhê yawan*) were succeeded by ('until the rise of') the Kittim. The name 'Kittim' is derived from the Phoenician words *kt* and *kty* which originally referred to Citium, a town in Cyprus near modern day Larnaca. In Jewish and Christian traditions, the name maintained a range of geographical and ethnic referents. In the Hebrew Bible, the term always occurred in the plural and was the name for the son of Javan, son of Japheth (Gen. 10.4; 1 Chron. 1.7), the island of Cyprus or the coastlands in general (Jer. 2.10; Ezek. 27.6). In 1 Maccabees 'Kittim' referred to the Greeks: Alexander the Great defeated the Persian King Darius after having marched from the 'land of the Kittim' (1.1); and in 168 BCE the Romans defeated not just Philip but also his son Perseus who

was the 'king of the Kittim' (8.5). References to the Kittim as Romans include the Aramaic and Latin translations of Num. 24.24 in Targum Onqelos and the Vulgate respectively, and the Greek translation of Dan. 11.30 in the Septuagint (*romaioi*). Josephus recognized the variety of designations when he explained that the name referred 'to all islands and to most maritime countries' (*Ant.* 1.128).

The name 'Kittim' occurs numerous times in the Qumran scrolls apart from 4QpNah (1QpHab 2.12, 14; 3.4, 9; 4.5, 10; 6.1, 10; 9.7; 1QpPs 9.4; 4QpIsa[a] 7-10.3.7, 9, 11, 12; 1QM 1.2, 4, 6, 9; 11.11; 15.9; 16.3, 6, 9; 17.12, 14; 18.2, 3; 19.10, 13; 4QM[a] 10.2.8, 10, 12; 11.2.8, 19; 13.5; 4QM[b] 1.9; 4Q285 5.6). Its identification with the Romans is based upon the above passage from 4QpNah and also the Habakkuk Pesher. In the exegesis of Hab. 1.16a in 1QpHab 6.1-5, the pesherist interpreted the biblical verse about the Chaldeans sacrificing to their net as a coded reference to the Kittim who 'sacrifice to their standards (*ototam*)', because 'their military arms are the objects of their reverence'. The veneration of their standards (*signa*) and weapons of war was a Roman practice. For instance, during the First Jewish Revolt and after Jerusalem had fallen, the Romans brought their standards into the Temple court, made sacrifices to them at the eastern gate, and there proclaimed Titus as Emperor (Josephus, *War* 6.316). It has also been suggested by several scholars that the Roman Senate may have been behind the reference to '[their] guilty house' in 1QpHab 4.10-13. In the pesher, it was according to the decision of this guilty house that '[their] rulers come [on]e after another to ruin the l[and]'.

Returning to 4QpNah, it is widely held that the phrase 'until the rise of the rulers of the Kittim' (frags. 3-4.1.3) refers to Pompey's intervention into the Jewish civil war and the capture of Jerusalem in 63 BCE. The historical context in view, then, would encompass a period from Antiochus Epiphanes (c. 170 BCE) to the Roman settlement of Palestine.

Though he did not develop it, Geza Vermes has put forward the suggestion that the Qumran community changed its mind about the Kittim (1994: 149). The earlier, neutral view is represented by the Habakkuk and Nahum Pesharim, whereas the later, hostile attitude can be seen in the War Scroll, War Rule (4Q285) and 4QpIsa[a] which considered the Roman force a Satanic army in the final eschatological battle. The Habakkuk pesherist depicted the Romans not in diabolical terms, but as instruments of divine punishment upon 'the last priests of Jerusalem' (1QpHab 9.4). Both 1QpHab (4.5, 10) and 4QpNah (3-4.1.2-3) describe the Kittim as being led by 'commanders' (*moshelim*) and not one ruler. In 4QpNah frags. 3-4.1.2-3 the contrast is striking in the use of royal terminology for Demetrius and Antiochus, but not for the commanders of the Kittim. But in the War Scroll, the leader who stands in front of the army of Belial against the sons of light is now 'the

King (*melek*) of the Kittim' (1QM 15.2). If correct this would mean that the Qumran scrolls witnessed the consolidation of political and military power under one man after the Battle of Actium (27 BCE) and considered him 'king', even if Augustus himself would have been reluctant to be so described. According to the latter view, then, the Kittim, who are identified with 'Lebanon' of Isa. 10.34 in 4Q161 7-10.3.7, will fall and their king will be put to death by the Prince of the Congregation (the 'him' of *heymito* of 4Q285 frag. 5.4).

The Kittim/Romans are characterized by the Habakkuk pesherist for their military might and ruthlessness. Like the Chaldeans of Habakkuk's prophecy, they are 'swift and mighty in war' (1QpHab 2.12-13) and 'merciless' (6.10-12), nations fear and dread them (3.4-5). Moreover, they lay siege to the fortresses of the nations (4.5-8), amass the booty of their conquered foes (6.1-2) and impose heavy, annual tributes upon all the peoples (6.6-8).

In the War Scroll, the name is qualified in two passages: 'the Kittim of Ashur' and 'the Kittim in Egypt' (1QM 1.4; 15.2-3; 19.10). It is possible that these references are not to the Romans, but to some other foreign army. It has been suggested that they are designations for the Seleucids and Ptolemies, although they may also have been terminological reflexes based upon the biblical texts in which both Ashur and the Kittim occur together several times.

1.2. The Wicked Priest

In his discussion of the possible source of the traditions found in the Pesharim (see below), Philip R. Davies has sounded a cautionary note against the assumption that historical data can be read out of these sectarian biblical commentaries. The reference to Demetrius and the identification of the Kittim with the Romans, which he does not question, 'do not establish *a priori* that the *pesharim* have reliable information about the 'Teacher' or the 'Wicked Priest' or the 'Man of the Lie'" (1987: 90-91). It is possible that the pesharim contain reliable historical information, but the data must be tested. Davies, then, studied the sobriquets in the pesharim and Hodayot and provided the negative conclusion that questioned the common assumption that the pesharim contain reliable historical information or even pre-existent traditions of the sobriquets. This caution remains true today as it did in the late 1980s, though the recently published texts cited above, which were unavailable to Davies, do emphatically support the view that the scrolls and the Qumranians were concerned with real people and events.

Davies also articulated a method for reading historical data out of the pesharim: 'wherever there is presented as an interpretation of a biblical text information which is not derivable from the text but seems gratuitous, then that information may be regarded as potentially of historical value. At least, it must be regarded as having a basis independent of the biblical text' (1987: 92). Take, for instance, his treatment of the interpretation of Hab. 2.15 in 1QpHab. 11.2-7 (in Vermes' translation):

> *Woe to him who causes his neighbours to drink; who pours out his venom to make*
> *them drunk that he may gaze on their feasts* (2.15).
>
>   Interpreted, this concerns the Wicked Priest who pursued the Teacher of Righteousness to the house of his exile that he might confuse him with his venomous fury. And at the appointed time for rest, for the Day of Atonement, he appeared before them to confuse them, and to cause them to stumble on the Day of Fasting, their Sabbath of repose.

From this passage Davies noted that three significant items are not derived from the biblical lemma: (1) the exile of the Teacher of Righteousness; (2) the Wicked Priest's malicious attempt to cause them to stumble; and (3) to confuse them ('swallowing' in his translation; Heb. *l^{e}bal'am*). He then discussed the relationship of this passage to 1QH 12.11-12 (formerly col. 4), noting that while they share lexical similarities, the fact that the Wicked Priest is entirely absent from 1QH (and also CD) is problematic.

As discussed in Chapter 4, the reading 'their feasts' appears to have been shared exclusively by the Habakkuk Pesher and 1QH and is probably an exegetical variant. As such, it could contain historical information that reflect a calendrical dispute between the Qumran community and the Temple. But, of course, this reading is not just derivable from the lemma, it is part of the biblical quotation.

Another difficulty is Davies' claim that 'confusing' or 'swallowing' them (*l^{e}bal'am*) is one of the three items not 'extracted from the biblical text' (1987: 92). True, the verb is not found in Hab. 2.15, but the interpretation of this passage is clearly dependent upon the biblical text of Hab. 1.13 cited earlier in 1QpHab 5.8-9 ('Why do you heed traitors, but are silent when a wicked one swallows up [*b^e-bal'a*] one more righteous than he?'). There, the interpretation concerns the House of Absalom and the man of the Lie rather than the Wicked Priest, but as I pointed out elsewhere the Habakkuk pesherist does not always maintain the distinction between the two: both the Wicked Priest and Liar are condemned for their illicit building activity and both are identified with the figure of 'the wicked' in the biblical text (Lim 1993: 421-24 and 2000a: 50-51). Inner cross-referencing is an exegetical method attested elsewhere in pesher Habakkuk.

The methodological point formulated by Davies needs to be qualified. It is better to consider 'gratuitous' information or textually independent material in the pesherist comment as most probably containing historical data, but not to exclude other material that can also be derived directly or indirectly from the scriptural texts. It is in the nature of pesherite exegesis to read into the scriptural text allusions to contemporary figures and events. To disqualify categorically comments that are related to the biblical lemma is to exclude information that may be potentially significant. Each passage needs to be examined on its own merits for what historical information they can and cannot yield. The faint outlines of the figures standing behind some of the sobriquets can be built up by data of varying historical probabilities.

Davies claimed that critical study of the sobriquets found in the pesharim has barely begun (1987: 105). This criticism of Qumran scholarship is overstated, but it does point to the need for greater critical rigour. In the past fifty years of Qumran scholarship, the identification of the Wicked Priest has been dominated by the 'Maccabean theory' that posited the illegitimate accession of Jonathan or Simon Maccabee to the office of high priesthood as a definitive moment in the origins and history of the community. According to this view, 'the Wicked Priest' was the nickname that the Qumran community gave to one or the other of the Maccabean brothers who, despite being non-Zadokites, acceded to the office of the high priesthood. The issue of illegitimate accession, however, is not to be found in the scrolls themselves, but in 1 Maccabees. John Collins (1989) has shown that neither the Rule of the Community nor the Damascus Document treats this as an issue.

Frank Cross based his identification of Simon Maccabee upon the so-called 'Psalms of Joshua' at the end of 4QTest (4Q175; 1995: 112-18). This passage, consisting of the biblical verse of Josh. 6.26 and its interpretation, which was quoted from a text that the community considered authoritative (namely 'the rewritten Joshua' [4Q379 frag. 22, col. 2]; see Newsom 1988), was interpreted by Cross as a reference to Simon Maccabee and his two sons, Judas and Mattathias. Geza Vermes alternatively argued that the Qumran community originally supported this illegitimate sacerdotal figure, as evidenced by the phrase that he was called 'by the name of truth at the beginning of his elevation' (1QpHab 8.9), but later demonized him as 'the Wicked Priest' and 'Liar' when he defiled the Temple and sinned against the Teacher of Righteousness and his followers (1987: 24-25).

Important developments in the investigation into the identity of the Wicked Priest occurred in the 1960s. Although anticipated in his conclusions by others, Gert Jeremias's seminal Heidelberg dissertation convinced many scholars that the sobriquets 'the Wicked Priest' (*Der Frevelpriester*) and 'the Liar' (*Der Lügenmann*) referred to two separate individuals, rather than one person: the high priest, probably Jonathan Maccabee, and a rival teacher within the Qumran community (1963: 36-126).

In his 'published' but not 'printed' 1971 Bonn dissertation, Hartmut Stegemann investigated the origin of the Qumran community. Emphasizing the relationship between the various opponents of the Teacher of Righteousness, he agreed with Jeremias that the Wicked Priest and Liar were separate individuals (1971: 41-53, 95-115).

Though they differed in important details, these scholars concurred that the one called 'the Wicked Priest' was a single individual. The designation 'the Wicked Priest' (*ha-kōhēn hā-rāshāʿ*) is a pun on the Hebrew title for 'the high priest' (*ha-kōhēn hā-rōš*) and occurs five times in the pesharim (1QpHab 8.8; 9.9 and 11.4 and once in 4QpPsᵃ 1-10.4.7-10). 1QpHab 8.16 and 9.16 have sometimes been included in addition to these five, but the phrases, 'the priest who rebelled...' and 'the [priest] who...', are badly mutilated. The reconstruction of '[the Wicked Priest]' in 1QpHab 1.13 is often followed, but as I have shown this restoration is highly questionable and a better reading would be: '[Its interpretation: *the wicked* is the man of the lie and *the righteous*] is the Teacher of Righteousness'(Lim 2000a). It is also widely held that the Wicked Priest spied on the Teacher of Righteousness and attempted to put him to death on account of the precepts and laws that the latter sent to him (4QpPsᵃ 1-10.4.7-10).

In 1988 an alternate hypothesis was proposed by Florentino García Martínez and Adam S. van der Woude called 'the Groningen Hypothesis'. According to this Dutch theory, the Qumran community was one of two daughter sects which split off from the mother community of the Essenes. The sect that settled at Qumran parted company with the larger group on account of the Teacher of Righteousness' eschatological and halakhic interpretation of the biblical texts. This schism was dramatically played out in the scene where the Liar, a rival teacher of the law, confronted the Teacher of Righteousness in the midst of their community (1QpHab 5.9-12). This is a theory still in the making, but a substantial portion of it has already been formulated in a preliminary fashion (for a discussion of it see Lim 1992a: 462-66).

The Groningen Hypothesis also considers the Wicked Priest and Liar as two separate individuals. Distinctively, the appellation 'the Wicked Priest' is regarded as a title that applied not to one individual, but a series of high priests in largely sequential order. According to van der Woude, who was the originator of this view, in four of the last five columns of the Habakkuk Pesher the title 'the Wicked Priest' refers to Judas Maccabeus (*de facto* high priest; 8.8-13), Alcimus (8.16–9.2), Jonathan (9.9-12), Simon (9.16–10.5), John Hyrcanus I (11.4-8) and Alexander Janneus (11.12–12.10). Aristobulus I, however, is omitted from this list for the dubious reason that he reigned for only one, short year.

The difficulties of this multiple priests theory are complex and have been set out in detail in Lim (1993). Van der Woude has replied and the following summary should be read alongside and compared to his responses (van der Woude 1996).

First, the identification of the sixth wicked priest with Alexander Jannaeus, whom van der Woude believed to have been contemporaneous with the

Habakkuk pesherist, is based upon two questionable grammatical points: (1) compared to the first five wicked priests who are qualified by a relative clause (*'ašer*), the last one is allegedly described in absolute terms. This, of course, contradicts the plain sense of 1QpHab 12.2-5 where the relative clause ('whom God will judge for destruction') comes after some intervening comments; (2) the use of the imperfect with this sixth wicked priest apparently indicates that his punishment was to come and not that it has already occurred. However, the imperfect is also used in 9.5 not just in the habitual, but also future, eschatological sense ('at the end of days their wealth together with their booty will be given into the hand of the army of the Kittim', 9.6).

Secondly, the complex argument that Judas Maccabeus *could* have been seen by the Qumran community to be functioning as *de facto* high priest is based primarily upon one of two accounts in Josephus and one reading of 2 Macc. 14.26. Josephus reported that the high priesthood was transferred to Judas after the death of Alcimus in *Ant.* 12.10.6; 12.314, 419, 434, but contradicted himself later in *Ant.* 20.237 when he stated that the office of the high priest remained unoccupied for seven years following Alcimus's death.

Similarly, 'his successor' in 2 Macc. 14.26 is one of two readings in the textual tradition. The NRSV translated the verse as follows:

> But when Alcimus noticed their goodwill for one another, he took the covenant that had been made and went to Demetrius. He told him that Nicanor was disloyal to the government, since he had appointed that conspirator against the Kingdom, Judas, to be his successor.

Following the Lucianic recension, Latin versions and the Venetian manuscripts, the NRSV translated the Greek as 'his successor'. In the central LXX witnesses, however, the reading is 'his kingdom' and the verse means: 'since he had appointed that conspirator against his Kingdom, Judas, to be successor'. The possessive pronoun 'his' would qualify 'kingdom' and not 'successor'. Moreover, even if, for the sake of argument, it is granted that 'his successor' is to be preferred, the most likely antecedent of the possessive would be Nicanor or Demetrius and not Alcimus.

Finally, the identification of the fourth wicked priest to be Simon in 1QpHab 9.16–10.5 runs into difficulties for several reasons: (1) the mutilated text of 9.16 preserves part of the word for 'the pr[iest]', but not 'the Wicked Priest'; (2) the passage is strikingly similar to the following one about the spouter of lies in 10.5–11.1, as both allude to illicit building activity; and (3) the pesherist comments are unspecific and may apply to any one of the Hasmonaean high priests.

Despite these difficulties, the multiple wicked priests theory of the Groningen Hypothesis appears to be 'on the right track' in suggesting that more than one figure stands behind the sobriquet (see also Brownlee 1982 and more recently Tantlevski 1995). It does not, as is often claimed, posit six wicked priests 'in strict sequential order' (since Aristobulus I is omitted). What the pesherist said about 'the Wicked Priest' is either too general or specific. The vices of avarice, inebriation and violence could apply to several of or all those who held the pontifical office (e.g. 1QpHab 9.6–10.5). Yet the passage about the Teacher of Righteousness reposing in his house of exile seems to refer to a particular occasion when a sacerdotal figure, known by the negative appellation of 'the Wicked Priest', appeared to him there (1QpHab 11.4-8), but it has no external corroboration. There is no evidence of any Maccabean or Hasmonaean high priest venturing to the Judaean Desert and the site of Khirbet Qumran. Nor is the attempt on the life of the Teacher of Righteousness by the Wicked Priest (4QpPsᵃ frags. 1-10.4.8-9) mentioned elsewhere. This murderous intent was apparently enacted because of 'the law that he [i.e. the Teacher of Righteousness] sent to him [i.e. the Wicked Priest]'. True, 4QMMT does enumerate some twenty or so laws between the 'we' and 'you' parties, but none of the points of dispute is serious enough to engender a criminal offence. The conciliatory tone of 4QMMT rules it out as 'the law' of 4QpPsᵃ.

All that is said about the Wicked Priest in the Habakkuk Pesher is unsuitable for the one figure of Jonathan or Simon. For example, the death of the Wicked Priest by a bitter affliction does not fit at all well with the sudden execution of Jonathan at the hands of Trypho. The drunken state of the Wicked Priest, described in 1QpHab 11.12-15, is a more appropriate description of Alexander Janneus's inebriation (Josephus, *Ant.* 13.398) than the habitual conduct of Jonathan or Simon. To be sure, Simon and his sons were killed by Ptolemy during a drunken banquet (1 Macc. 16.1-17), but it is unclear whether they were customarily given to drink.

There are indicators within the Habakkuk Pesher that more than one high priest was envisioned. In 1QpHab 9.4-7, it mentions 'the last priests of Jerusalem' who plunder the people, but who will be handed over to the army of the Kittim/Romans at the end of days. This fits well with the presumed date of the composition of pesher Habakkuk (c. 60–50 BCE). Moreover, the plurality of wicked priests is suggested by the irreconcilably different ways by which each figure comes to an end (by the hand of his enemies, 9.8-12; by divine punishment, 10.3-5; by bodily affliction, 11.12-15 and 8.16–9.2).

1.3. The Liar
There is no consensus that the Liar was a personality distinct from the Wicked Priest. The main proponents of the Maccabean theory believe that the two are one and the same. As mentioned, the Habakkuk pesherist did not always keep the two separate. The commentator of 4QpPsᵃ seems to have done something similar, identifying the 'wicked one' of Ps. 37.32-33

with the Wicked Priest (frags. 1-10.4.7-10) and 'a wicked one' two verses later (vv. 35-36) with 'the [M]an of the Lie' (frags. 1-10.4.13-15). Although for him, the biblical figures of the wicked have a wider range of referents: they are also 'the ruthless ones of the covenant' (frags. 1-10.2.13-16; 3.8-13; 4.1-2; 4.18-21?), 'the wicked ones of Ephraim and Manasseh' (frags. 1-10.2.16-20), and all who do not go out with the congregation of the chosen ones (frags. 1-10.3.2-5; 4.10-12?).

Other scholars follow Gert Jeremias in seeing a rival pedagogue in the sobriquet 'the Liar' or 'the man of the lie' (*'ish ha-kāzāv* 1QpHab 2.2; 5.11; 11.[1]; CD 20.15) and its variant appellation, 'the spouter (or preacher) of the lie' (*maṭṭîp ha-kāzāb*; 1QpHab 10.9; 1Q14 10.[2]; CD 8.13 = 19.26). The insult 'the scoffer' (*'îš ha-lāšôn*) also seems to have been a name for the liar, since he too is described as one who 'dripped (*hiṭṭîp*) over Israel waters of lie' (CD 1.14). The image of dripping (*ntp*) words as a form of false teaching is found in the biblical texts (Mic. 2.6, 2.11; Amos 7.16, 9.13). It is the glib teaching of the false prophet who seduces the people with words that flow like wine and honey. Those described as 'scoffers of Jerusalem' in 4Q162 2.6 are likely to have been a group associated with the liar.

According to 4QpPs[a] 1-10.1.25-27, many were led astray by the deceitful words of this liar and chose frivolous things over the words of the 'interpreter of knowledge' (*melits da'at*), most likely a reference to the Teacher of Righteousness. In an interpretation of Hos. 4.16 in CD 1.14-17, it is said that:

> the Scoffer arose who shed over Israel waters of lies. He caused them to wander in a pathless wilderness, laying low the everlasting heights, abolishing the ways of righteousness and removing the boundary with which the forefathers had marked out their inheritance, that he might call down on them the curses of His Covenant and deliver them up to the avenging sword of the Covenant.

Prior to the publication of the 4Q copies of the Damascus Document, it was often thought that this entire section was secondary to CD 1 (e.g. Davies 1987: 70). It may still be so, but its antiquity is evidenced by the partially preserved parallel in 4Q266, frag. 2, col. 1, lines 17-18. Much of this description can be traced to one biblical source or another, but it is generally agreed that this insertion has the effect of particularizing the introductory admonition to the rival group of the community (CD 1.1-13; so Knibb 1987: 16-26). Philip Davies has suggested the intriguing thesis that the pesherists drew general terms from the Hodayot and infused them with specific meaning. Thus, the plurality of figures charged as 'the interpreters of false-hood' in the Hodayot become the singular 'man of the lie' in the pesharim (1987: 99-100).

For Florentino García Martínez and the late Adam van der Woude, it was a fundamental difference in the matter of interpreting the law that led to the

schism between those who followed the inspired Teacher of Righteousness
to Qumran and those who stayed faithful to the leader of the Essenes,
known only by the disparaging insult, 'the liar' (García Martínez 1988: 124-
25). The exegesis of Hab. 1.13b in 1QpHab 5.9-12 preserves the dramatic
encounter between the rival teachers (in García Martínez's translation):

> Its prediction concerns the House of Absalom and the members of its council
> who were silent at the time of the reproof of the Teacher of Righteousness and
> gave him no help against the Liar who flouted the Law in the midst of their
> whole [congregation].

This passage has often been explained as the House of Absalom and the
members of its council remaining guiltily silent at the time of the Teacher of
Righteousness' reproof. Although his own translation does not bring it out,
García Martínez in fact holds to a slightly different view: 'The basic elements
of the pesher are that the Liar 'rejects the Law' in the midst of all the community…and that the majority of this community accepts the position of the
Liar until the just rebuke of the Teacher of Righteousness reduces them to
silence' (1988: 125). This interpretation of the events has been independently
confirmed by Hugh Williamson (1977–78) who argued on linguistic grounds
that the plural niphal verb, *ndmw*, should be translated in the passive, 'were
reduced to silence', in effect rendering the 'reproof' of the Teacher of Righteousness as a subjective genitive. It was the Teacher who not only opposed
the man of the lie but it was also his rebuke that reduced the House of
Absalom and the men of their congregation to silence.

1.4. The Teacher of Righteousness
The sobriquet 'the Teacher of Righteousness' translates the Hebrew expression *moreh ha-ṣedeq*, a phrase which is derived from Joel 2.23, *ha-moreh li-
ṣedaqah*. The sense of the biblical verse, however, is obscure: what does it
mean for Yahweh to have given the children of Zion 'early rain' for their
vindication and why should this act become a cause for rejoicing? The term
môrêh is based on the root *yrh* and means 'early rain' in contrast to 'later rain'
(*malqôš*) and the same word can also mean 'teacher'. The way that the Qumran community understood Joel 2.23 is in the context of other biblical texts
that combine the notion of rain and righteousness with teaching. In Hos.
10.12, the prophet summoned sinful Israel 'to seek the Lord, that he may
come and rain righteousness (*yôrê ṣedeq*) upon you'.

The life-sustaining effect of rain is a literal and figurative consequence of
the moral and legal conduct of Israel. Solomon's petitionary prayer in 1 Kgs
8.35-36 (cf. 2 Chron. 6.26-27) expresses this connection both in the confes-
sion of sin, 'When heaven is shut up and there is no rain (*māṭār*) because
they have sinned against you', and in the invocation of forgiveness, 'then

hear in heaven, and forgive the sin of your servants, your people Israel, when you teach them (*tôrēm*) the good way in which they should walk'. In Isa. 30.19-26, there is a reference to a 'teacher' in the Lord's promise to be gracious to Zion: 'your Teacher (*môrêkhâ*) will not hide himself any more, but your eyes shall see your Teacher (*môrêkhâ*). And when you turn to the right or when you turn to the left, your ears shall hear a word behind you, saying, "This is the way; walk in it"' (vv. 20-21). Associated with this is that God 'will give rain (*māṭār*) for your seed' (v. 23).

Joel 2.23 is often translated as 'for he has given the early rain for your vindication [*ha-môrêh li-ṣedāqâ*]', but the Qumran community understood the verse to mean that God has given 'the Teacher' who will direct them 'for righteousness'. Though the sobriquet is most often expressed as *môrê ha-ṣedeq* 'the Teacher of Righteousness', there is a variant form that uses the synonym of Joel 2.23, *môrê ha-ṣedeqâ* (1QpHab 2.2). The absolute form of *môrê ṣedeq* in CD 1.11 and 20.32 does not mean that there was 'a Teacher of Righteousness'; the omission of the definite article may be explained by the poetic context in which the phrase is found. Other names for the same individual is *môrê ha-yaḥyd* or 'the unique teacher', which may have been an error for *môrê ha-yaḥad* or 'teacher of the community' (CD 20.1, 14), *dôrēš ha-tôrâh* or 'the interpreter of the law' (CD 6.7) and *mēlîṣ da'at* 'the interpreter of knowledge' (4QpPsᵃ 1-10.1.27). In CD 6.10-11, there is a strikingly similar phrase, 'until he comes who shall teach righteousness (*yôrêh ha-ṣedeq*) at the end of days', but it appears that he is a messianic figure to come and not the Teacher of Righteousness—who is already referred to as 'the interpreter of the law' in the same passage. 'The messiah of righteousness' in 4QCommentary on Genesis A 5.3 appears to be the same eschatological figure.

Only 5 of the 800 or so scrolls from Qumran mention the Teacher of Righteousness, 4 of these are pesharim (1QpMic, 1QpHab, 4QpPsᵃ, 4QpPsᵇ) and the fifth is the Damascus Document. The references in 1QpMic and 4QpPsᵇ are too fragmentary to be of any use. Direct knowledge of this unique individual, therefore, is confined to three texts. Much has already been said above and in previous chapters about the central role that the Teacher of Righteousness plays in the interpretation of law and Scripture. Here, it should be added that Teacher of Righteousness is widely held to be the founding member of the Qumran community. The beginning of the admonitions section of CD 1.1-11 provides the historical origins of the Qumran community and the role that the Teacher played:

> Listen now all you who know righteousness, and consider the works of God; for He has a dispute with all flesh and will condemn all those who despise Him.

> For when they were unfaithful and forsook Him, He hid His face from Israel and His Sanctuary and delivered them up to the sword. But remembering the Covenant of the forefathers, He left a remnant to Israel and did not deliver it up to be destroyed. And in the age of wrath, three hundred and ninety years after He had given them into the hand of King Nebuchadnezzar of Babylon, He visited them, and He caused a plant root to spring from Israel and Aaron to inherit His Land and to prosper on the good things of His earth. And they perceived their iniquity and recognized that they were guilty men, yet for twenty years they were like blind men groping for the way.
>
> And God observed their deeds, that they sought Him with a whole heart, and He raised for them *the* Teacher of Righteousness to guide them in the way of His heart.

Much ink has been spilt on this passage, not least in attempting to understand the chronology of the movement referred to as 'a plant root' (cf. 1 Macc. 2.42; 7.13; 2 Macc. 14.6). A literal enumeration will produce a date of 177 BCE (i.e. 587 – 390 – 20), but as it is often pointed out the 390 and 20 years respectively are symbolic figures. The former symbolically represents the period of punishment in Ezek. 4.5 and the latter is half of the exemplary number of 40. It is noteworthy that proponents of the Maccabean theory need to set aside the literal value of the figures in place of a rough reckoning. There is, in fact, no positive, numerical evidence for dating the emergence of the remnant to 150 BCE in CD 1. The Teacher of Righteousness, then, appears to have been the re-founder of a reform party that had been 'groping for the way' for the past 20 years. In 4QpPs^a frags. 1-10.3.16, the comment on Ps. 37.23-24 states that God had 'established him to build for Him a congregation of [his chosen ones in truth]'.

The Qumran community regarded the Teacher of Righteousness as the priest (*ha-kohen*, 1QpHab 2.8; 4QpPs^a frags 1-10.3.15) who was chosen to interpret the prophetic oracles for contemporary life. In the interpretation of Hab. 2.3 in 1QpHab 7.4-5, he is also identified with the prophet Habakkuk who was commanded by Yahweh to aid readers' understanding of the vision by writing it down. This prophetic tradition is evident when his utterance is described as having come 'from the mouth of God' (1QpHab 2.2), a phrase used with the biblical prophets ('in the book of Zechariah from the mouth [of God], 4QpIsa^c frags. 1-10.8). The Teacher of Righteousness is not explicitly referred to as 'prophet', but in his hermeneutical role he does follow the prophetic tradition. Faithfulness to the teachings of the Teacher of Righteousness guaranteed both compliance with the perceived will of God and a member's place in the salvific plan (1QpHab 8.2).

The divinely inspired prophetic interpretation of the Teacher of Righteousness was carried forward by his followers. It is likely that the Teacher *par excellence* of the Qumran community, following biblical tradition, established the pesher-form of exegesis. In 1QpHab 2.8 his divine commission to interpret the prophetic oracles is expressed with the verbal form of the technical term *lipšōr*. The Teacher of Righteousness probably taught orally, given the emphasis upon his speech and repeated mention of the 'hearing' of those around him, a pedagogical pattern more in accord with the practices of the Jewish and Graeco-Roman world. His followers, however, wrote biblical commentaries. It is an assumption that the two techniques are identical.

It is held by a number of scholars that either he penned some of the hymns or that the person referred to as 'I' in the Hodayot is the Teacher of Righteousness. As long ago as 1955, E. Sukenik had posited that the Hodayot or Thanksgiving Psalms express the thanks and complaint of an individual who may be identified with the Righteous Teacher (1955: 39). Specifically, the phrase 'he thrusts me out of my land like a bird from its nest' (1QH 12.9 [formerly col. 4]) corresponds to the exile of the Teacher of Righteousness in 1QpHab 11.6. Subsequent form-critical studies of the Hodayot, however, have distinguished two groups of hymns: those that express the individual thanksgiving songs (*individuelle Danklieder*) and other hymns (*hymnische Bekenntnislieder*) (G. Morawe 1961 and Holms-Nielsen 1960). The form-critical study of the Hodayot has now reached a high level of sophistication (see the recent dissertations of Douglas 1998 and Chum 2000) and the recently published copies of the Hodayot from Cave 4 (see now the principal editions in E. Schuller, DJD, 29) are likely to complicate rather than simplify the task.

There are general affinities between the Hodayot and the sectarian texts on the concepts of eschatological war, predeterminism, dualism between good and evil and the final judgment. More specific similarities are compared between passages from the 1QHodayot and the pesharim.

> 1QH 10.9-11 (formerly col. 2): you made me an object of insult and derision to the traitors, but a counsel of truth and understanding to the upright of way. I was the cause of the iniquity of the wicked, a source of whispering on the lips of the **ruthless**; the scoffers ground their **teeth**. (Knibb translation)
>
> 4QpPs[a] frags 1-10.2.13-16: *The wicked plots against the righteous and gnashes* [*his teeth*] *at* [*him.*] *Yahweh laughs at him, for he sees that his day has come* (Ps. 37.12-13). The interpretation of it concerns the **ruthless ones** of the covenant who are in the house of Judah: they will plot to destroy completely those who observe the Law, who are in the council of the community. But God will not abandon them into their power. (Horgan translation)

Of the two terms hightlighted above, the mention of 'teeth' is less important, since it occurs in the biblical lemma, than 'the ruthless ones' (*'arîṣîm*). The 'traitors' (*bōgedîm*) of 1QH moreover figure in 1QpHab 2.1-10, CD 1.12; 8.5 and 19.17.

It is possible that the Teacher of Righteousness may have written some of the hymns of individual thanksgiving. But as Sukenik observed long ago and the observation has subsequently been demonstrated, the whole of the Hodayot imitates the style of the biblical psalms. In fact, it has often been remarked that although the Thanksgiving Psalms quotes a biblical text only once, virtually every line of the text is replete with biblical phrases and allusions. In such a situation, great care should be exercised in reading historical information out of these texts.

In CD 20.14, there is a reference to the 'gathering in' of the Teacher of Righteousness. The phrase 'to gather in' (to his family) is a common expression for death (e.g. Gen. 25.8, 17). It is, therefore, widely held that the Teacher of Righteousness died, but the suggestion that he returned from the dead has few supporters. Also, the claim that he died at 40 is unsubstantiated and based upon a misunderstanding of the passage. In CD 20.13-14, the 40 year period occurs from the death of the Teacher of Righteousness to the apostasy of 'the men of war' with the Liar.

There have been many attempts to identify the Teacher of Righteousness, from Onias III (c. 175 BCE) to John the Baptist, Jesus or James. The Christian interpretations are ruled out by the dating of 4Q266 and 1QpHab before the Christian period (see Knibb 2000: 920-21). It is possible that the Teacher of Righteousness was not only a priest, but held the office of high priest. As mentioned above, in one account of Josephus, it is said that the pontifical office remained vacant for seven years between the death of Alcimus and the accession of Jonathan Maccabee (159–152 BCE). It is, of course, impossible for the high priestly office to remain unoccuppied for a lengthy period, given the central role that he played in cultic ritual and sacrifice, including the day of atonement, so it has been suggested that the Teacher of Righteousness was the high priest who occupied the office those seven years and whose name was later erased from the records because of his dissent against appointing a non-zadokite high priest in Jonathan.

2. 1Q Hodayot as a Source for the Pesharim

In a chaper subtitled, 'The Life of the 'Teacher' in Hymn and Pesher', Philip Davies has proposed the intriguing thesis that the pesharim drew many of its traditions about the historical figures from the Hodayot (*Behind the Essenes*, pp. 87-105). He examined the literary affinity between 1QpHab 11.2-8 and 1QH 12.5-12 and six sobriquets and terms ('violent or ruthless', 'lie or falsehood', 'seekers of smooth things', 'simple', 'poor' and 'interpreters of knowledge by wonderful mysteries'), concluding that what the pesharim say about the Teacher of Righteousness is not historically reliable, since the data seem to be based upon the Hodayot. Terms that are non-specific in 1QH are adapted and applied by the pesherists to the biblical texts. They are secondary and at best would describe traditions about the Teacher of Righteousness, similar to ascriptions about Jesus in the New Testament, rather than the historical person himself.

This thesis needs to be thoroughly tested. Here, it will suffice to make a few points. First, the copies of the Hodayot from Cave 4 need to be included in the discussion. They were not available to Davies, but have now been published as principal editions in DJD, 29. Second, 1QH itself is clearly dependent upon other texts, especially the Psalms, but other biblical and non-biblical sources as well. Both 1QH and a recently published sapiential text called 4QInstruction or *mûsār le-mēvîn* share at least one verse (1QH 10.27-28 and 4Q418, frag. 55, 10). The relationship between these two texts needs to be explored. Third, there is inadequate attention paid to the biblical quotations and textual traditions that they may or may not share with extra-Qumran material. Mention has already been made of the exclusive reading of 'their feasts' between the Habakkuk pesher and 1QH.

In the opposite direction, the tradition about the 'ruthless ones' (*'aritsim*) in the Hodayot, 1QpHab and 4QpPs[a] needs to be seen in the wider context of shared textual traditions. 1QpHab 2.1-10 is a passage that interprets Hab. 1.5 as a reference to the 'ruthless [ones of the covenant]' and this may well be based upon the references to 'violent men' in 1QH. However, it is also based upon the textual variant of 'the traitors' (*ha-bogedim*). The description 'ruthless [ones of the covenant]' is another name for '[the trai]tors' in 1QpHab 2.5-6. In this form, it is a textual variant externally corroborated in the LXX and Acts as the following show:

MT (lit):	look at the nations (*ba-gōyîm*) and see
1QpHab 1.16-17:	lemma badly mutilated and uncertain of reading.
1QpHab 2.3:	commentary includes 'trai[tors]' (*ha-bōgᵉdîm*)
LXX:	'traitors' (*hoi kataphronētai*)
Acts 13.41	citing Hab. 1.5: 'traitors' (*hoi kataphronētai*)

It is not clear whether the original lemma would have cited the variant 'traitors'. Whether it did or not, is not vital since the pesherist does interweave other variants into his commentary. A thorough investigation into the sobriquets should include a close study of the biblical quotations (cf. Hab. 2.5 and the use of *bōgēd*).

3. Imitating the Prophetic Style

The combination of allusions and explicit historical references in Pesher Nahum correlates well with the style of the biblical prophecy. The oracles of Nahum are directed against Assyria and the city of Nineveh. Explicit references to both are found in 'an oracle concerning Nineveh' (1.1), 'Nineveh is like a pool' (2.9), 'Nineveh is devastated' (3.7) and 'King of Assyria (*melek aššûr*). But the nation and her people are also 'lions' (*'arāyôt, kᵉphîr*) in 2.11-13, an allusion to her might as depicted on Assyrian reliefs.

Interestingly, the neo-Babylonians in the prophecy of Habakkuk are not explicitly mentioned as such. The phrase for 'the Babylonians' in 2 Kgs 17.30 is *'anše bābel*. The code used in the prophecy is the name often associated with them, 'the Chaldeans' (*ha-kaśdîm*; 1.6). The Habakkuk pesher does not make explicit references to the Romans, but likewise uses a term that is closely, but not exclusively, associated with them.

6

PESHER AND THE NEW TESTAMENT

The genre of Pesher was directly applied to the exegesis of many parts of the New Testament, especially those of Matthew and Paul. A prominent example is Krister Stendahl's study (1954) of the so-called 'formula quotations' (an English synonym for the German *Reflexionscitate*), a group of some twenty quotations of the Old Testament text in the Gospel of Matthew, that are characterized by the introductory formula 'in order that it may be fulfilled'. He argued that in these quotations there contained 'material of the *pesher* type, which was intended for the theology and teaching of the church' (1954: 195-96). Stendahl followed William Brownlee in defining the Qumran commentary of Habakkuk as a 'midrash pesher' (1954: 184).

Likewise, E. Earle Ellis has argued that Paul's interpretation of the Old Testament is essentially a midrash pesher (1957; 1978: 173-81; 1969; 1988: 691-726). The explanation of a textual variant cannot account for several phenomena found in the explicit citations of the letters. The underlying rationale in Paul's usage, both in its textual manifestations and theological applications, is to be found in the exegetical moulding of the biblical text. The problem is essentially one of interpretation and this interpretation is none other than the so-called 'midrash pesher' which is also found in the Gospels of Matthew and John.

Though dependent upon the expertise of Qumran scholars (1969: 64), Ellis explained that the midrash pesher: (1) merges pertinent verses into one strongly expressive 'prooftext'; (2) adapts their grammar to the New Testament context and application; (3) chooses appropriate renderings from known texts or targumim; and (4) creates *ad hoc* interpretations. Illustrating this method, he argued that Paul has created or selected and inserted the phrase 'in victory' (*eis nikos*), also attested by Aquila and Theodotion but not the LXX ('strength'), into the merged quotation of Isa. 25.8 (cf. Hos. 13.14) in 1 Cor. 15.54-55 ('Death is swallowed up in victory. Where, O death, is your victory? Where, O death, is your sting?'), because the idea of death swallowed up in victory is so intimately connected with the victory of Christ's resurrection.

Similarly, C.K. Barrett (1970: 392) has suggested that Rom. 10.6-7 is a pesher when he transposed the Pauline passage to a putatively Qumran commentary form:

> Do not say in your heart, Who shall ascend into heaven? The *pešer* of this is, Who shall bring Christ down? Do not say in your heart, Who shall descend into the deep? The *pešer* of this is, Who shall bring Christ up from the dead?

The assumption here is that the Greek phrase *tout' estin* in Paul's text translates *pesher*. But this is imprecise; the lexical equivalent in the Hebrew of the pesharim is the use of the masculine or feminine independent pronoun, *hy'* or *hw'*, used with or without a demonstrative and substantive. For example, in 4QpIsa[b] 2.11, those who rejected the law in Isa. 5.24c-25 are identified with the scoffers of Jerusalem: 'This is [*hy'*] the congregation of the scoffers who are in Jerusalem'. Ellis also mistakenly equated the two expressions (1988: 696-97).

As discussed in Chapter 2, the term *pesher* has several meanings, ranging from the specific fulfillment of prophetic oracles, characteristic of sectarian exegesis, to identification-exegesis, a generic form of 'this is that'. Compare, for example, the similarities between two columns from 4Q252. Column 4, lines 3-6, interprets Gen. 49.3-4 with the pesher formula:

> The blessings of Jacob: Reuben, you are my firstborn and the first fruit of my strength, exceeding in destruction and exceeding in power. Unstable as water, you shall no longer exceed, (because) you went up to your father's bed. Then you defiled it. On his couch you went up (Gen. 49.3-4) [vacat] Its interpretation is that (*pišrô 'ašer*) he reproved him (i.e. Reuben) for having lain with Bilhah his concubine.

And col. 5, lines 1-5:

> *A ruler shall not depart from the tribe of Judah* (Gen. 49.10). When Israel will have the dominion, one sitting in it (i.e. the throne) for David will not be cut off. For the *staff* is the covenant of the kingdom, the clans of Israel are *the standards*, until the coming of the messiah of righteousness, the scion of David. For to him and his seed has been given the covenant of the kingdom to his people for eternal generations which he kept (Brooke translation, DJD, 17: 205).

The term is not to found in the latter passage, but the exegesis is similar to the interpretation of Gen. 49.3-4 in the previous column where *pišrî* is used (see Lim 2000b: 64; cf. Greek Esther 10.3).

The abstraction of the pesherite form of exegesis from the Qumran scrolls and its application to the New Testament's interpretation of the Old Testament raise numerous problems. Some twenty years ago, Matthew Black dismissed the supposed genre of midrash pesher 'as a modern invention probably best forgotten' (1971: 1). J.D.G. Dunn's description of pesher as 'a narrower form of midrash' (1977: 84-85), was rightly criticized by Larry Hurtado (1979: 136) and George J. Brooke (1979–80: 483-84), for being so vague as to be of little use.

The discussion of the pesher genre in Chapter 3 has questioned the basis for the continuing use of this hybrid genre, midrash pesher. The pesher is neither generic nor unique, but it is distinctive and this distinctiveness, both in structure and content, should not be homogenized into an undifferentiated Jewish-Christian biblical interpretation by its application to exegeses of the New Testament that may have some superficial similarities.

In any case, it is not clear what is to be gained by calling Pauline or Matthean exegesis 'a midrash pesher'. Both Paul and Matthew have their own concerns, hermeneutical principles and methods of scriptural exegeses and these are better illuminated within their own contexts.

1. Common Sectarian Matrix

The Qumran community, Essenes and Early Church are not one and the same community, nor did they belong generally to Second Temple Judaism. They circulated among the circles often described as 'sectarian'. The term 'sectarian' is badly in need of qualification, both in its assumption of separation from a larger body and the various sociological models that are embraced by the term. In any case, the Qumran community and New Testament writers drew on a common pool of tradition, first and foremost on the authoritative Scriptures which they shared with the rest of Judaism, and also some 'non-canonical' writings and oral traditions.

It is striking how many parallels can be drawn between the terminology and concept used in the Qumran scrolls and Pauline letters. Yet these parallels, when examined in context often turn out to be rather limited. This is true for the common use of the term 'New Covenant' of Jeremiah 31 fame for very different purposes: the scrolls interpret *berît ḥadāšâ* as a renewal of the old covenant, whereas Paul thought of *kainē diathēkē* as a new dispensation, christologically centred, and replacing 'the old covenant'. Both drew on the promise of restoration in Jeremiah 31 (38), whereas rabbinic literature virtually ignored it, except possibly in the case of circumcision. But while the Qumran community underscored the first part (until v. 32), contrasting the new covenant with that of the fathers, Paul emphasized vv. 33-34 and the internalization of the torah.

Or again, Paul and the Qumran scrolls drew on Ps. 142 (143).2 ('for no one living will be counted righteous before you'), but while the former applied it to the Gentiles as 'transfer terminology' (following E.P. Sanders), the latter used it in 1QS, 1QH and 4Q415ff to express the Jewish sense of the unattainable status of being in a right relationship with God (for this entire argument, see Lim 2002b).

Turning to the pesharim and related literature, this same pattern can be discerned. Take, for example, the interpretation of Isaiah 54 in frag. 1 of 4QpIsa[d], lines 1-7 which read as follows:

> *Behold, I will set your stones in antimony* (54.11b). [Interpreted, this saying concerns]...all Israel is like antimony surrounding the eye. *And I will lay your foundations with sapphires* (54.11c). Interpreted, this concerns the Priests and the people who laid the foundations of the Council of the Community...the congregation of His elect (shall sparkle) like a sapphire among stones.
> [*And I will make*] *all your pinnacles* [*of agate*] (54.12a). Interpreted, this concerns the twelve [chief Priests] who shall enlighten by judgement of Urim and Tummim...which are absent from them, like the sun with all its light, and like the moon...[*And all your gates of carbuncles*] (54.12b). Interpreted, this concerns the chiefs of the tribes of Israel...

As mentioned earlier, the rebuilding of the New Jerusalem of Second Isaiah was infused with a specifically sectarian reading that tied the hierarchical structure of the community to architectural features. The final chapters of the book of Revelation also drew on the common source of Isa. 54.11-12, but used it to describe the eschatological Temple/City of Jerusalem that will be constructed with precious stones (Rev. 21.18-21).

The Temple Scroll, 4QpNah and Galatians 3 also drew on the same source of Deuteronomy 21 but applied it to different forms of killing by hanging. Deuteronomy 21.22-23 read as follows in the NRSV:

> When someone is convicted of a crime punishable by death and is executed, and you hang him on a tree, his corpse must not remain all night upon the tree; you shall bury him that same day, for anyone hung on a tree is under God's curse.

Note the sequence of the punishment: execution, followed by hanging on a tree, then burial. The passage does not stipulate what these transgression were and the crimes covered under 'judgment of crimes punishable by death'. But it makes clear that it is the corpse that is impaled for humiliation.

In the Temple Scroll, col. 64.6-13, the word order of Deut. 21.23 is reversed, so that it reads 'and you shall hang him also upon the tree and he shall die'. Yigael Yadin argued that the hanging is an act that puts the man to death and related it to the 'hanging men alive' of 4QpNah, frags. 3-4, col. 1.7 (1983: I, 373-79). It is likely that 4QpNah referred to hanging as a form of crucifixion, given the historical context of Alexander Janneus and the rebellion led by the Pharisees. However, in the Temple Scroll it could be hanging at the end of a rope (so Baumgarten 1972).

When Paul quoted Deut. 21.23 as prooftext in Gal. 3.13, he was also referring to Jesus' crucifixion. But the theological significance that he drew from it is very different. Rather than a straightforward punishment for a crime, it became a divinely ordained plan so that 'in Christ Jesus the blessing of Abraham might come to the Gentiles' (v. 14; for a full discussion, see Lim 1997a: 164-68).

A final example is to be found in the centrality of Hab. 2.1-4 for both Paul and the Qumran pesherist. One of the pivotal prooftexts, Hab. 2.4 expressed for the apostle the theological belief that righteousness for Gentiles came from faith: 'the one who is righteous will live by faith' (Gal. 3.11; cf. Rom. 1.17; but a different form in Heb. 10.37-38). That faith, of course, was in Christ Jesus. In the prophecy of Habakkuk, 2.4 included the significant possessive 'his': 'the righteous live by *his* faith'. This faith, of course, was the faithfulness of the righteous Israelite, in contrast to the proud. His faithfulness was predicated on the assurance that another vision for the appointed time will surely come despite being late.

In 1QpHab 7.17–8.3, the faithful Israelite of Hab. 2.4 (lemma mutilated) was identified with all those of the 'house of Judah who observe the Law' and whom God will save from judgment on account of their tribulation and fidelity to the Teacher of Righteousness. In the Qumran context, it is not just observing the law that is important, but also faithfulness to its teachings as interpreted by the Righteous Teacher. The context of the Habakkuk pesherist's comment is particularly interesting. As discussed in Chapter 2, the structure of the pesher shows that the first four verses of Habakkuk 2 form the pivotal hermeneutical passage for the pesherist's own understanding of the role of the Teacher of Righteousness and the tradition that he is following (1QpHab 6.12–8.3). Again, Paul and the pesherist hit upon the same text, but drew different lessons from it.

The Qumran community and the Early Church belonged to the common sectarian matrix and not to Second Temple Judaism generally. This explains both the numerous lexical and terminological affinities that they share, their quotation of the same biblical source texts, and the similarities and differences in their interpretations. They were not identical and the historical link between them is possible, but in any case they must have lived in similar circles.

Bibliography

Abegg, M., Jr, P. Flint and E. Ulrich
    1999   *The Dead Sea Scrolls Bible* (New York: HarperSanFrancisco; Edinburgh: T. & T. Clark).

Alexander, P.S.
    1983   'Rabbinic Judaism and the New Testament', *ZNW* 74: 237-46.
    1984   'Midrash and the Gospels', in C.M. Tuckett (ed.), *Synoptic Studies: The Ampleforth Conferences of 1982 and 1983* (Sheffield: JSOT Press): 1-18.
    1993   'A Note on the Syntax of 4Q448', *JJS* 44: 301-302.
    2000   'The Bible in Qumran and Early Judaism', in A.D.H. Mayes (ed.), *Text in Context. Essays by Members of the Society for Old Testament Studies* (Oxford: Oxford University Press): 35-62.

Allegro, J.
    1964   *The Dead Sea Scrolls: A Reappraisal* (Harmondsworth: Penguin Books).

Allegro, J.M. and A.A. Anderson
    1968   Qumrân Cave 4. I (4Q158–4Q186) (DJD, 5; Oxford: Clarendon Press): 11-15, pls. IV-V.
    1956   'Further Messianic References in Qumran Literature', *JBL* 75: 177-82, pls. II and III.

Amoussine, J.D.
    1969–71 'Observantiunculae qumraneae', *RevQ* 7: 533-52.

Aranda Perez, G., F. García Martínez and M. Perez Fernandez
    1996   *Literatura judia intertestamentaria* (Estella, Navarra: Editorial Verbo Divino).

Avigad, N.
    1958   'The Palaeography of the Dead Sea Scrolls and Related Documents', in *Aspects of the Dead Sea Scrolls* (Jerusalem: Magnes Press): 56-78.

Baigent, M., and R. Leigh
    1991   *The Dead Sea Scrolls Deception.* (London: Corgi). Vatican conspiracy suggested and Robert Eisenman's interpretation of the scrolls popularized.

Barrett, C.K.
             'The Interpretation of the Old Testament in the New', in P.R. Ackroyd (ed.), *Cambridge History of the Bible. I. From the Beginnings to Jerome* ed. (Cambridge: Cambridge University Press, 1970): 377-411.

Baumgarten, J.M.
    1972   'Does TLH in the Temple Scroll Refer to Crucifixion?', *JBL* 91: 472-81.

1992   'The Disqualification of Priests in 4Q Fragments of the "Damascus Document", a Specimen of the Recovery of pre-Rabbinic Halakha' in *MQC*: II, 503-14.

Baumgarten, J.M. *et al.*
1999   *Qumran Cave 4: Halakhic Texts* (DJD, 35; Oxford: Clarendon Press).

Beall, T.S.
1988   *Josephus' description of the Essenes Illustrated by the Dead Sea Scrolls* (Cambridge: Cambridge University Press).

Berger, K.
1995   *Jesus and the Dead Sea Scrolls: The Truth under Lock and Key?* (ET J.S. Currie; Louisville, KY: Westminster/John Knox Press). Response to Michael Baigent and Richard Leigh *Dead Sea Scrolls Deception* (1991) and significance for Christianity considered.

Bergmeier, R.
1993   *Die Essener-Berichte des Flavius Josephus: Quellenstudien zu den Essenertexten im Werk des Jüdischen* Historiographen (Kampen: Kok Pharos Publishing House).

Bernstein, M.
1993–94   '4Q252 i 2 לא ידור רוחי באדם לעולם: Biblical Text or Biblical Interpretation', *RevQ* 16: 421-27.

1994   'Introductory Formulas for Citation and Re-Citation of Biblical Verses in the Qumran Pesharim', *DSD* 1: 30-70.

2000   'Pesher Habakkuk' in *EDSS*: II, 647-50.

Berrin, S.L.
        'Pesharim', in *EDSS*: II, 644-47.

Betz, O., and R. Riesner
1994   *Jesus, Qumran and the Vatican* (ET J. Bowden; London: SCM Press). Refutation of Michael Baigent and Richard Leigh, *Dead Sea Scrolls Deception* (1991) and alternative Early Church connection argued.

Birnbaum, S.A.
1957a   *The Hebrew Script*. I. *The Texts* (Leiden: E.J. Brill).
1957b   *The Hebrew Script*. II. *The Plates* (London: Paleographia).

Black, M.
1971   'The Christological Use of the Old Testament in the New Testament', *NTS* 18: 1-14.

Bonani, G., M. Broshi, I. Carmi, S. Ivy, J. Strugnell and W. Wolfi
1991   'Radiocarbon dating of the Dead Sea Scrolls' *'Atiqot* 20: 27-32. Report of the Zurich laboratory carbon 14 testing of 8 Qumran scrolls (4QTQahat, 4Q365, 1QIsaᵃ, 4QTLevi, 4QSamᶜ, 11QTemple and 1QApGen), 2 Masada texts and 4 documents from Wadi Daliyeh, Wadi Seyal, Murabbaʿat and Khirbet Mird.

Brooke, G.J.
1979–80   'Qumran Pesher: Towards the Redefinition of a Genre', *RevQ* 10: 483-503.

1985   *Exegesis at Qumran: 4QFlorilegium in its Jewish Context* (Sheffield: JSOT Press).

1987   'The Biblical Texts in the Qumran Commentaries: Scribal Errors or Exegetical Variants?', in C.A. Evans and W.F. Stinespring (eds.), *Early*

Jewish and Christian Exegesis: Studies in Memory of William Hugh Brownlee (Atlanta: Scholars Press): 85-100.

1990   'Pesher', in R.J. Coggins and J.L. Houlden (eds.), *A Dictionary of Biblical Interpretation* (London: SCM Press): 531-32.

1996   *Qumran Cave 4. XVII: Parabiblical Texts, Part 3* (DJD, 22; Oxford: Clarendon Press, 1996): 185-207, pls. XII-XIII.

2000a   '*E Pluribus Unum*: Textual Variety and Definitive Interpretation in the Qumran Scrolls', in T.H. Lim *et al.* (eds.), *The Dead Sea Scrolls in their Historical Context* (Edinburgh: T. & T. Clark): 107-22.

2000b   'Catena', in *EDSS*: II, 121-22.

2000c   'Florilegium', in *EDSS*: II, 297-98.

Broshi, M.

1998   'Ptolas and the Archelaus Massacres (4Q468g = 4QHistorical Text B)', *JJS* 49: 341-45.

Brownlee, W.H.

1951   'Bible Interpretation among the Sectaries of the Dead Sea Scrolls', *BA* 19: 54-76.

1955   'The Habakkuk Midrash and the Targum of Jonathan', *JSS* 7: 169-86.

1959   *The Text of Habakkuk in the Ancient Commentary from Qumran* (JBL Monograph Series, 11; Philadephia: SBL, 1959).

1979   *The Midrash Pesher of Habakkuk* (Missoula, MT: Scholars Press).

1982   'The Wicked Priest, the Man of Lies, and the Righteous Teacher: The Problem of Identity', *JQR* 73: 1-37.

Bruce, F.F.

1959   *Biblical Exegesis in the Qumran Texts* (The Hague: Vitgeverij va Keule N.V.).

Burrows, M., J.C. Trever and W.H. Brownlee

1950   *The Dead Sea Scrolls of St Mark's Monastery. I. The Isaiah Manuscript and the Habakkuk Pesher* (New Haven: American Schools of Oriental Research).

Callaway, P.R.

1988   *The History of the Qumran Community: An Investigation* (Sheffield: JSOT Press).

Carmignac, J.

1963   *Les Textes de Qumran: traduits et annotes* (2 vols.; Paris: Letouzey et Ané).

1969–71   'Le Document de Qumrân sur Melkisédeq', *RevQ* 7: 342-78.

Chum, B.

2000   'A Literary Analysis of 1QH 10-17 :36', PhD, University of Edinburgh.

Collins, J.J.

1989   'The Origins of the Qumran Community: A Review of the Evidence' in M.P. Horgan and P.J. Kobelski (eds.), *To Touch the Text: Biblical and Related Studies in Honor of Joseph A. Fitzmyer, S.J.* (New York: Cross-road): 159-78.

1997   *Apocalypticism in the Dead Sea Scrolls* (London: Routledge).

Cook, E.M.

1994   *Solving the Mysteries of the Dead Sea Scrolls* (Carlisle: Paternoster Press).

Cross, F.M.
1961   'The Development of the Jewish Scripts', in G.E. Wright (ed.), *The Bible and the Ancient Near East: Essays in Honor of W.F. Albright* (New York: Doubleday): 144-202.
1992   'Some Notes on a Generation of Qumran Studies', in *MQC* 1: 1-14.
1995   *The Ancient Library of Qumran* (Sheffield: Sheffield Academic Press, 3rd edn). Classic introduction revised.

Cross, F.M. and E. Eshel
1997   'Ostraca from Khirbet Qumrân', *IEJ* 47: 17-28.

Davies, P.R.
1987   *Behind the Essenes: History and Ideology in the Dead Sea Scrolls* (Atlanta: Scholars Press).
1996   *Sects and Scrolls: Essays on Qumran and Related Topics* (Atlanta: Scholars Press).

de Jonge, M., and A.S. van der Woude
1966   '11QMelchizedek and the New Testament', *NTS* 12: 301-26.

de Vaux, R.
1973   *Archaeology and the Dead Sea Scrolls* (ET D. Bourke; Oxford: Clarendon Press).

Dimant, D.
1984   'Qumran Sectarian Literature', in M.E. Stone (ed.), *Jewish Writings of the Second Temple Period: Apocrypha, Pseudepigrapha, Qumran Sectarian Writings, Philo, Josephus* (Assen: Van Gorcum; Philadelphia: Fortress Press): 483-550.
1992   'Pesharim, Qumran' in *ABD*: V, 244-51.

Doudna, G.
1998   'Dating the Scrolls on the basis of radiocarbon analysis', in *The Dead Sea Scrolls after Fifty Years* (ed. James C. VanderKam and Peter Flint; Leiden: E.J. Brill): 430-71.

Douglas, M.C.
1998   'Power and Praise in the Hodayot: A Literary Critical Study of 1QH 9.14-18.14', PhD, University of Chicago.

Driver, G.R.
1965   *The Judaean Scrolls: The Problem and a Solution* (Oxford: Basil Blackwell).

Duhaime, J.
1990   *Les Esséniens de Qumrân—des Ésotéristes?* (La Corporation des Éditions Fides). Discussion of modern religious movements inspired by Essenism.

Dunn, J.D.G.
1977   *Unity and Diversity in the New Testament* (London: SCM Press)

Dupont-Sommer, A.
1970–71   'Résumé des cours de 1969–70', *Annuaire du Collège de France 70* (Montreal): 399-414.

Eisenman, R.
1996a   *James the Brother of Jesus: The Key to Unlocking the Secrets of Early Christianity and the Dead Sea Scrolls* (New York: Viking). The Jamesian hypothesis offered.
1996b   *The Dead Sea Scrolls and the First Christians* (Shaftesbury: Element). Collection of previously published works and other writings.

Eisenman, R. and M. Wise
    1992   *The Dead Sea Scrolls Uncovered* (Shaftesbury: Element). Controversial
                translation of then unpublished Qumran texts.
Elliger, K.
    1953   *Studien zum Habakuk-Kommentar vom Toten Meer* (Tübingen: J.C.B.
                Mohr). Seminal studies emphasizing the revelatory nature of the Habak-
                kuk Pesher.
Ellis, E.E.
    1957   *Paul's Use of the Old Testament* (London: Oliver & Boyd).
    1969   'Midrash, Targum and New Testament', in E.E. Ellis and M. Wilcox
                (eds.), *Neotestamentica et Semitica: Studies in Honour of Matthew Black*
                (Edinburgh: T. & T. Clark, 1969): 61-69.
    1978   *Prophecy and Hermeneutic in Early Christianity: New Testament Essays.*
                (WUNT, 18; Tübingen: J.C.B. Mohr).
    1988   'Biblical Interpretation in the New Testament Church', in M.J. Mulder
                and H. Sysling (eds.), *Mikra. Text, Translation, Reading and Interpretation
                of the Hebrew Bible in Ancient Judaism and Early Christianity* (Assen: Van
                Gorcum; Philadelphia: Fortress Press): 691-726.
Eshel, E.
    1994   'The Rebukes by the Overseer', *JJS* 45: 111-22.
Eshel, E., and M. Stone
    1995   *Qumran Cave 4. XIV: Parabiblical Texts, Part 2* (DJD, 19; Oxford:
                Clarendon Press): 215-30, pl. XXIX.
Eshel, E., H. Eshel and A. Yardeni
    1992   'A Qumran Composition containing part of Ps. 154 and a Prayer for the
                Welfare of King Jonathan and his Kingdom', *IEJ* 42: 199-229.
Feltes, H.
    1986   *Die Gattung des Habakukkommentars von Qumran (1QpHab): Eine
                Studie zum frühen jüdischen Midrasch* (Würzburg: Echter Verlag).
Finkel, A.
    1963–64   'The Pesher of Dreams and Scriptures', *RevQ* 4: 357-70.
Fishbane, M.
    1988   'Use, Authority and Interpretation of Mikra at Qumran', in M.J. Mulder
                and H. Sysling (eds.), *Mikra. Text, Translation, Reading and Interpretation
                of the Hebrew Bible in Ancient Judaism and Early Christianity* (Assen:
                Van Gorcum; Philadelphia: Fortress Press): 339-78.
Fitzmyer, J.A.
    1992   *Responses to 101 Questions on the Dead Sea Scrolls* (London: Geoffrey
                Chapman). Brief and sensible answers to complex questions.
Gabrion, H.
    1979   'L'interprétation de l'Ecriture dans les littérature de Qumrân', *Aufstieg
                und Niedergang der Römischen Welt* (New York: W. de Gruyter): II.19.1,
                779-848.
García Martínez, F.
    1988   'Qumran Origins and Early History: A Groningen Hypothesis', *Folia
                Orientalia* 25: 113-36.
García Martínez, F.
    1994–95   *The Dead Sea Scrolls Translated: The Qumran Texts in English* (Leiden:
                E.J. Brill).

García Martínez, F. and J. Barrera Trebolle

    1995   *The People of the Dead Sea Scrolls: Their Writings, Beliefs and Practices* (ET W.G.E. Watson; Leiden: E.J. Brill). Miscellaneous collection of articles by two leading Spanish scholars.

García Martínez, F., and E.J.C. Tigchelaar

    1997–98   *The Dead Sea Scrolls Study Edition.* I. *(1Q1-4Q273).* II. *(4Q274-11Q31)* (Leiden: E.J. Brill). Facing Hebrew/Aramaic and English edition.

García Martínez, F., E.J.C. Tigchelaar and A.S. van der Woude

    1998   *Qumran Cave XI, 11Q2-18, 11Q20-31* (DJD, 23; Oxford: Clarendon Press): 221-41, pl. XXVII.

García Martínez, F., and A.S. van der Woude

    1990   'A 'Groningen' Hypothesis of Qumran Origins and Early History', *RevQ* 14: 521-42.

Golb, N.

    1995   *Who Wrote the Dead Sea Scrolls? The Search for the Secret of Qumran* (London: Michael O'Mara). Jerusalem hypothesis advanced.

Greenfield, J.

    1988   'The Words of Levi Son of Jacob in Damascus Document IV, 15-V, 10)', *RevQ* 49-52: 319-22.

Harnack, A.

    1958   *A History of Dogma* (ET; New York: Russell & Russell).

Hatch, E.

    1889   *Essays in Biblical Greek* (Oxford: Clarendon Press).

Hendel, R.S.

    2000   'Scriptures: Translations', in *EDSS*: II, 836-39.

Holm-Nielsen, S.

    1960   *Hodayot: Psalms from Qumran* (Aarhus: Universitetsforlaget).

Horbury, W.

    1999   'The Proper Name in 4Q468g: Peitholaus?', *JJS* 50.2: 308-309.

Horgan, M.P.

    1979   *Pesharim: Qumran Interpretations of Biblical Books* (Washington: Catholic Biblical Association of America): 70-86; Texts: 15-19.

Jeremias, G.

    1963   *Der Lehrer der Gerechtigkeit* (Göttingen: Vandenhoeck & Ruprecht, 1963). Seminal study in identifying the Wicked Priest and Liar as two different figures.

Jull, A.J.T., D.J. Donahue, M. Broshi and E. Tov

    1996   'Radiocarbon Dating of the Scrolls and Linen Fragments from the Judean Desert', *'Atiqot* 28: 85-91. Report of the Arizona laboratory carbon 14 testing of 15 Qumran scrolls (4Q266, 1QpHab, 1QS, 4Q258, 4Q171, 4Q521, 4Q267, 4Q249, 4Q317, 4Q208, 4Q22, 4Q342, 4Q344, 4Q345, 1QIsaᵃ), three documents from Naḥal Hever and two samples of textiles from Cave 4 and Wadi Murabba'at.

Kister, M.

    1992   'Biblical Phrases and Hidden Biblical Interpretations and *Pesharim*' in D. Dimant and U. Rappaport (eds.), *The Dead Sea Scrolls: Forty Years of Research* (Leiden: E.J. Brill): 27-39.

Knibb, M.A.

    1987   *The Qumran Community* (Cambridge: Cambridge University Press.

Contains translated extracts with commentary on some of the most important scrolls.

2000 'Teacher of Righteousness', in *EDSS*: II, 918-21.

Lemaire, A.

1997a 'Le Roi Jonathan à Qoumrân (4Q448, B-C)', in E.-M. Laperrousaz (ed.), *Qoumrân et les Manuscrits de la mer Morte. Un cinquantenaire* (Paris: Les Editions du Cerf): 57-70.

1997b 'Qoumrân: sa fonction et ses manuscrits', in E.-M. Laperrousaz (ed.), *Qoumrân et les Manuscrits de la mer Morte. Un cinquantenaire* (Paris: Les Editions du Cerf): 117-49.

Lim, T.H.

1990 'Eschatological Orientation and the Alteration of Scripture in the Habakkuk Pesher', *JNES* 49: 185-94.

1991 *Attitudes to Holy Scripture in the Qumran Pesharim and Pauline Letters* (DPhil dissertation, Oxford).

1992a 'The Qumran Scrolls: Two Hypotheses', *SR* 21.4: 455-66. Examines the Jerusalem and Groningen Hypotheses.

1992b 'The Chronology of the Flood Story in a Qumran Text (4Q252)', *JJS* 43: 288-98.

1993 'The Wicked Priests of the Groningen Hypothesis', *JBL* 112/3: 415-25.

1997a *Holy Scripture in the Qumran Commentaries and Pauline Letters* (Oxford: Clarendon Press).

1997b 'Midrash Pesher in the Pauline Letters', in S.E. Porter and C.A. Evans (eds.), *The Scrolls and Scriptures* (Sheffield: Sheffield Academic Press): 280-91.

2000a 'The Wicked Priest or the Liar?', in T.H. Lim *et al.* (eds.), *The Dead Sea Scrolls in their Historical Context* (Edinburgh: T. & T. Clark): 45-51.

2000b 'The Qumran Scrolls, Multilingualism, and Biblical Interpretation', in J.J. Collins and R.A. Kugler (eds.), *Religion in the Dead Sea Scrolls* (Grand Rapids: Eerdmans): 57-73.

2000c 'Kittim', in *EDSS*: I, 469-71.

2000d 'Liar', in *EDSS*: I, 493-94.

2000e 'Wicked Priest', in *EDSS*: II, 973-76.

2000f 'Paul, Letters of', in *EDSS*: II, 638-41.

2001a 'An Alleged Reference to the Tripartite Division of the Hebrew Bible', *RevQ* 77: 23-37.

2001b Review of *The Dead Sea Scrolls Bible* by M. Abegg, Peter Flint and Eugene Ulrich, *JTS* 52.2 (1999): 759-61.

2002a 'Biblical Quotations in the Pesharim and the Text of the Bible: Methodological Considerations', in E.D. Herbert and E. Tov (eds.), *The Bible as Book: The Scripture at Qumrant* (London: The British Library).

2002b 'Studying Paul and the Qumran Scrolls in their Historical Context', in J.R. Davila (ed.), *The Dead Sea Scrolls as Background to Postbiblical Judaism and Early Christianity* (Leiden: E.J. Brill).

Lim, T.H. in consultation with P.S. Alexander

1997 *The Dead Sea Scrolls Electronic Reference Library Volume 1* (Oxford: Oxford University Press; Leiden: E.J. Brill). Digitized images of all the Dead Sea Scrolls with bibliographical annotations.

Lohse, E.
  1964   *Die Texte aus Qumran: Hebräisch und deutsch* (Munich: Kösel-Verlag).
              Facing Hebrew (with masoretic pointing) and German texts.
Manns, F.
  1990   *Le Midrash. Approche et Commentaire de* L'Ecriture (Jerusalem).
Martin, M.
  1958   *The Scribal Character of the Dead Sea Scrolls* (Louvain: Universitè de
              Louvain Institut Orientaliste).
Milik, J.T.
  1955   *Qumran Cave I* (Oxford: Clarendon Press): 77-80, pl. XV.
  1959   *Ten Years of Discovery in the Wilderness of Judaea* (ET J. Strugnell; Lon-
              don: SCM Press). Dated, but still basic introduction.
  1972   'Milkî-sedeq et Milkî-reša' dans les anciens écrits juifs et chrétiens', *JJS*
              23: 109-26.
Miller, M.P.
  1971   'Targum, Midrash and the Use of the Old Testament in the New
              Testament', *JSJ* 2: 29-82.
Molin, G.
  1952   'Der Habakukkomentar von 'En Fešha in der alttestamentlichen Wissen-
              schaft', *TZ* 8.5: 340-56.
Morawe, G.
  1961   *Aufbau und Abgrenzung der Loblieder von Qumrân: Studien zur gattungs-
              geschichlichen Einordnung der Hodajoth* (Berlin: Evangelische Verlags-
              anstalt).
Neusner, J.
  1987   *What is Midrash?* (Philadelphia: Fortress Press).
Newsom, C.
  1988   'The "Psalms of Joshua" from Cave4', *JJS* 39: 56-73.
Niehoff, M.
  1992   'A Dream Which is not Interpreted is Like a Letter Which is not Read',
              JJS 43: 58-84.
Nitzan, B.
  1986   *Pesher Habakkuk: A Scroll from the Wilderness of Judaea (1QpHab)*
              (Heb.) (Jerusalem: Bialik Institute).
Oppenheim, A.L.
  1956   'The Interpretation of Dreams', *Transactions of the American Philological
              Association* 46: 179-355.
Pfann, S. (ed.)
  1999   *Qumran Cave 4. Halakhic Texts*, DJD, 35 (ed. J. Baumgarten *et al.*;
              Oxford: Clarendon Press).
Pietersma, A.
  2000   *A New English Translation of the Septuagint: The Psalms* (Oxford: Oxford
              University Press).
Puech, E.
  1987   'Notes sur le manuscrit de XIQMelkîsédeq', *RevQ* 12/48: 483-513.
  1993   *La Croyance des Esséniens en la vie future: immortalité, résurrection, vie
              éternelle? Histoire d'une croyance dans le judaïsme ancien* (Paris: Etudes
              Bibliques).

Rabin, C.
1955   'Notes on the Habakkuk Scroll and the Zadokite Documents', *VT* 5: 148-62.

Rabinowitz, I.
1973   'Pêsher/Pittaron: Its Biblical Meaning and its Significance in the Qumran Literature', *RevQ* 8: 219-32.

Rengstorff, K.H.
1960   *Hirbet Qumran und die Bibliothek vom Toten Meer* (Stuttgart: Kohl-hammer).

Rodley, G.A. and B. Thiering
1999   'Use of Radiocarbon Dating in Assessing Christian Connections to the Dead Sea Scrolls', *Radiocarbon* 41.2: 169-82. Arguing that radiocarbon dates do correlate with a Christian interpretation of the scrolls.

Schiffman, L.H.
1993   'Pharisees and Sadducees in Pesher Nahum', in M. Bettler and M. Fishbane (eds.), *Minha le-Nahum: Biblical and Other Studies Presented to Nahum M. Sarna in Honour of His Seventieth Birthday* (Sheffield: JSOT Press): 272-90.

Schuller, E. *et al.*
1999   *Qumran Cave 4. XX. Poetical and Liturgical Texts, Part 2* (DJD, XXIX: Oxford: Clarendon Press).

Schürer, E., G. Vermes, F. Millar, M.D. Goodman *et al.*
1973–87 *History of the Jewish People in the Age of Jesus Christ* (Edinburgh: T. & T. Clark): I-III.2.

1994   *Reclaiming the Dead Sea Scrolls: Their True Meaning for Judaism and Christianity* (Philadelphia: Jewish Publication Society). Sadducean theory espoused.

2000   'Halakhah and Sectarianism in the Dead Sea Scrolls', in T.H. Lim *et al.* (eds.), *The Dead Sea Scrolls in their Historical Context* (Edinburgh: T. & T. Clark): 123-42.

Schwartz, D.
1999   '4Q468g: Ptollas?', *JJS* 50.2: 308-309.

Seeligmann, I.L.
1953   'Voraussetzungen der Midraschexegese', in *Congress Volume, Cophenhagen, 1953* (VTSup, 1; Leiden: E.J. Brill): 150-81.

Segert, S.
1953–55 'Zur Habakuk-Rolle aus dem Funde vom Toten Meer I-IV', *Archiv Orientalni* 21: 218-39; 22 (1954): 99-113, 444-459; 23 (1955): 178-83, 364-73 and 575-619.

Shanks, H. (ed.)
1992   *Understanding the Dead Sea Scrolls* (New York: Random House). Popular articles on scrolls and controversies.

Silberman, L.H.
1961   'Unriddling the Riddle: A Study in the Structure and Language of the Habakkuk Pesher', *RevQ* 3: 323-64.

Sinclair, L.A.
1983   'Hebrew Text of the Qumran Micah Pesher and Textual Traditions of the Minor Prophets', *RevQ* 11: 253-63.

Slomovic, E.

1969 'Toward and Understanding of the Exegesis of the Dead Sea Scrolls', *RevQ* 9: 3-15.

Stegemann, H.

1967 'Weitere Stücke von 4QPsalm 37, von 4QPatriarchal Blessings und Hinweis auf eine unedierte Handschrift aus Höhle 4Q mit Exzerpten aus dem Deuteronomium' *RevQ* 6: 211-17.

1971 *Die Entstehung der Qumrangemeinde*, Bonn doctoral dissertation.

1992 'The Qumran Essenes: Local Members of the Main Jewish Union in the Late Second Temple Times', in *MQC*: II, 83-166. *MQC* Vol. 2: 83-166.

1993 *Die Essener, Qumran, Johannes der Täufer und Jesus* (Freiburg: Herder).

Stendahl, K.

1954 *The School of Matthew and its Use of the Old Testament* (Lund: C.W.K. Gleerup).

Steudel, A.

1990 'Eschatological Interpretation of Scripture in *4Q177 (4QCatena^a)*', *RevQ* 14.3: 473-81.

1992 '*4QMidrEschat: «A Midrash on Eschatology»* (4Q174 +4Q177)', in *MQC*: II, 531-41.

1993 '*'aharit ha-yamim* in the Texts from Qumran', *RevQ* 61/16: 225-246

1994 *Der Midrasch zur Eschatologie aus der Qumrangemeinde (4QMidrEschat^{a,b}): Materielle Rekonstruktion, Textebestand, Gattung und traditionsgeschichtliche Einordnung der durk 4Q174 ('Florilegium') und 4Q177 ('Catena A') repräsentierten Werkes aus den Qumranfunden* (Leiden: E.J. Brill): 5-56.

Strugnell, J.

1969–71 'Notes en marge du volume V des Discoveries in the Judaean Desert of Jordan' *RevQ* 7: 183-86.

Sukenik, E.L. (ed.)

1955 *The Dead Sea Scrolls of the Hebrew University* (Jerusalem: Magnes Press).

Talmon, S.

1951 'Yom Hakkippurim in the Habakkuk Scroll', *Biblica* 32: 549-63.

Tantlevskij, I.R.

1995 'The Two Wicked Priests in the Qumran Commentary on Habakkuk' *The Qumran Chronicle* 5, Appendix C.

Thiering, B.

1992 *Jesus the Man* (London: Doubleday) (=*Jesus and the Riddle of the Dead Sea Scrolls* [San Francisco: Harper Collins, 1992]). Unconvincing use of pesher method to reveal the alleged true meaning of the Gospels.

1996 *Jesus of the Apocalypse: The Life of Jesus after the Crucifixion* (London: Doubleday).

Tov, E.

1986 'The Orthography and Language of the Hebrew Scrolls Found at Qumran and the Origin of these Scrolls', *Textus* 13: 31-57. Theory of Qumran morphology advanced.

1992 *Textual Criticism of the Hebrew Bible* (Minneapolis: Fortress Press; Assen: Van Gorcum).

1999 *The Dead Sea Scrolls Electronic Reference Library*. Volume 2. Prepared by the Foundation for Ancient Research and Mormon Studies. Including 'The Dead Sea Scrolls Database (Non-Biblical Texts) (Leiden: E.J. Brill Academic Publishers).

Tov, E. with the collaboration of S.J. Pfann
1993   *The Dead Sea Scrolls on Microfiche* (Leiden: E.J. Brill).

Ulrich, E.
1999   *The Dead Sea Scrolls and the Origins of the Bible* (Grand Rapids: Eerdmans).
2000   'The Qumran Biblical Scrolls: The Scriptures of Late Second Temple Judaism' T.H. Lim *et al.* (eds.), in *The Dead Sea Scrolls in their Historical Context* (Edinburgh: T. & T. Clark): 67-87.

VanderKam, J.C.
1994   *The Dead Sea Scrolls* Today (Grand Rapids: Eerdmans; London: SPCK). Accessible introduction.

van der Kooij, A.
2000   'Textual Witnesses to the Hebrew Bible and the History of Reception: The Case of Habakkuk 1.11-12', in U. Damien, A. Lange and H. Lichtenberger (eds.), *Die Textfunde vom Toten Meer und der Text der Hebräischen Bibel* (Vluyn: Neukirchener Verlag): 91-108.

van der Ploeg, J.
1951   'Le Rouleau d'Habacuc de la grotte de 'Ain Fešha', *BO* 8: 2-11.

van der Woude, A.S.
1965   'Melchisedech als himmlische Erlösergestalt in den neugefundenen eschatologischen Midraschim aus Qumran Höhle XI' *OTS* 14: 354-73.
1982   'Wicked Priest or Wicked Priests? Reflections on the Identification of the Wicked Priest in the Habakkuk Commentary', *JJS* 33: 349-59.
1996   'Once Again: The Wicked Priests in the Habakkuk Pesher from Cave 1 of Qumran', *RevQ* 17: 375-84.

Vegas Montaner, L.
1980   *Biblia del Mar Muerto: Profetas Menores: Edición crítica según manuscritos hebreos procedentes del Mar Muerto* (Madrid: Instituto 'Arias Montano').
1989   'Computer-Assisted Study on the Relation between 1QpHab and the Ancient (Mainly Greek) Biblical Versions', *RevQ* 14: 307-23.

Vermes, G.
1961   *Scripture and Tradition in Ancient Judaism* (Leiden: E.J. Brill).
1976   'Interpretation, History of. B. At Qumran and in the Targums', IDBSup: 438-43.
1987   *The Dead Sea Scrolls in English* (London: Penguin Books, 3rd edn).
1989   'Bible Interpretation at Qumran', *EI* 20: 184-91.
1993   'The So-called King Jonathan Fragment (4Q448)', *JJS* 44: 294-300.
1994   *The Dead Sea Scrolls: Qumran in Perspective* (London: SCM Press, rev. edn). Classic introduction now updated.
1997   *The Complete Dead Sea Scrolls in English* (London: Penguin Books, 5th edn).

Vermes, G. and M. Goodman
1989   *The Essenes According to the Classical Sources* (Sheffield: JSOT Press). Facing Greek-English translations of Josephus, Philo, Pliny and others on the Essenes.

Vermes, G., T.H. Lim and R.P. Gordon

    1992   'The Oxford Forum for Qumran Research: Seminar of the Rule of War from Cave 4 (4Q285)', *JJS* 32: 86-90.

Wagner, S.

    1960   *Die Essener in der Wissenschaftlichen Diskussion vom Ausgang des 18. bis zum Beginn des 20. Jahrhunderts* (Berlin: Verlag Alfred Töpelmann).

Weiss, R.

    1963   'A Comparison between the Massoretic and the Qumran Texts of Nahum III, 1-11' *RevQ* 4: 433-49.

White, R.T.

    1990   'The House of Peleg in the Dead Sea Scrolls', in P.R. Davies and R.T. White (eds.), *A Tribute to Geza Vermes: Essays on Jewish and Christian Literature and History* (Sheffield: JSOT Press): 67-98.

Wieder, N.

    1953   'The Habakkuk Scroll and the Targum', *JJS* 4: 14-18.

Wise, M., M. Abegg and E. Cook

    1996   *The Dead Sea Scrolls: A New* Translation (San Francisco: HarperSanFrancisco). Recent English translation on the scrolls.

Welhausen, J.

    1898   *Die Kleinen Propheten. Übersetz und Erklärt* (Berlin: Verlag von Georg Reimer 3rd edn).

Williamson, H.G.M.

    1977–78   'The Translation of 1QpHab V, 10', *RevQ* 9: 263-65.

Yadin, Y.

    1983   *The Temple Scroll* (2 vols.; Jerusalem: Israel Exploration Society).

Yardeni, A.

    1998   'Breaking the Missing Link', *BARev* 24.3: 44-47.

INDEXES

INDEX OF REFERENCES

BIBLE